# The Queen and I

Discovery Books

# The
# Queen
# and I  *STUDIES IN ESTHER*

## Ray C. Stedman

*WORD BOOKS, Publisher*
*Waco, Texas*

THE QUEEN AND I

Quotations from the Revised Standard Version of the
Bible, copyrighted 1946, 1952, © 1971, 1973
by the Division of Christian Education of the National
Council of the Churches of Christ in the United States
of America, are reprinted by permission.

Discovery Books are published by Word Books,
Publisher, in cooperation with Discovery Foundation,
Palo Alto, California.

ISBN 0–8499–0015–8
Library of Congress catalog card number: 77–075471
Printed in the United States of America

First Printing – September, 1977
Second Printing – April, 1978

# CONTENTS

First: A Key 7

A Pair of Queens 16

The Struggle for Control 25

The Crafty Foe 33

Divine Grief 42

The Dinner That Delays 55

The Price of Survival 64

Haman's Last Supper 73

The Law of the Spirit 83

The Sweet Taste of Victory 93

# Chapter 1

# FIRST: A KEY

Tucked away in the Bible in an obscure corner of the Old Testament is the little book of Esther. It is a delightful story of human love and palace intrigue set in the days of Israel's captivity under the Median-Persian Empire. It tells of a captive Jewish maiden who, through an amazing series of incidents, was elevated to the throne of Persia as its queen, and how God used her position of power and authority to preserve his people against a Hitler-like attack. Even to this day the Jews celebrate the feast of Purim in memory of this deliverance accomplished through Queen Esther.

But for many this little book is a puzzle, for it seems to be out of place in the Bible. There is no mention in it of the name of God; there is no reference to worship or to faith; there is no prediction of the Messiah; there is no mention of heaven or hell—in short, there is nothing religious about it, at least on the surface. It is a gripping tale, but one might rather expect to find it in the pages of the Reader's Digest than the Bible. The best that many commentators can make of it is to view it as a revelation of God's providence—the way he works behind the scenes to preserve his people in times of peril.

Such a view is certainly a valid approach to Esther. The book does beautifully unfold the ability of God to work through natural means and to bring about his will through the free choices of men who are unconscious of coercion, but there is more to it even than that. The real key to the book lies in the New Testament.

The apostle Paul makes clear in several of his letters that the historic incidents that happened to Israel are intended as types or parables for us. They occurred so that we might have an illustration of what God intends to do with us. This does not mean that these accounts are stylized legends of unhistoric events. They really happened! But, in the wisdom of God, they happened in such a way as to form a detailed picture of God's dealings with us on a spiritual level. The Old Testament is thus God's visual aid to the truth of the New Testament.

Paul could write to the Corinthians, "Now these things happened to them as a warning (actually the word is "as types"), but they were written down for *our* instruction, upon whom the end of the ages has come" (1 Cor. 10:11, emphasis added). And again to the Romans he says, "For whatever was written in former days was written for *our* instruction, that by steadfastness and by the encouragement of the scriptures we might have hope" (Rom. 15:4, emphasis added). If we learn to read Old Testament stories using this key from the New Testament, we will discover that these stories are far more than mere history. They are highly practical accounts of what is happening to us on our own spiritual journey.

If we take the authentic history of the book of Esther in this light, we shall find it a living parable of exquisite and accurate insight. Jesus frequently taught by parables, laying one truth alongside another to illuminate and explain it. He used the Old Testament in this way, indicating that the days of Noah were a picture of world conditions at the time of his second coming, and that the experience of Jonah in the fish's belly was a foreview of his death and resurrection. The very first parable God ever devised for man's instruction was to take a rib from Adam's side and make a woman and lay her alongside him. When Adam looked into Eve's face he saw a reflection of his own life. Man has been busy trying to interpret that parable ever since and has come up with some rather remarkable explanations of it. It is still a great mystery!

### The Mystery of Us

To understand the book of Esther, then, we shall look for the story behind the story, for only thus will the book come to life for us. We shall discover that the story of this book is really our story, that what happens here is happening also in our lives. In the unfolding of this story we shall find an unfolding also of the mystery of our own makeup. The greatest mystery to man is man himself. The Bible is given to us not only that we may learn to know God, but that we may also learn to know ourselves. There is no book in the Bible more helpful to this end than Esther.

The story centers around a kingdom and its king. It opens with a report of the magnificence of that kingdom.

In the days of Ahasuerus, the Ahasuerus who reigned from India to Ethiopia over one hundred and twenty-seven provinces, in those days when King Ahasuerus sat on his royal throne in Susa the capital, in the third year of his reign he

he gave a banquet for all his princes and servants, the army
chiefs of Persia and Media and the nobles and governors of
the provinces being before him, while he showed the riches
of his royal glory and the splendor and pomp of his majesty
for many days, a hundred and eighty days. (Esther 1:1-4)

Perhaps you might be startled to learn that the name of
this king is never given to us. The word Ahasuerus is not a
personal name; it is a title, like Czar or Emperor. It means
"The Venerable Father," an apt title indeed for a king.
Many Bible scholars identify this king with Xerxes the Great
who led the Persian armies against the power of Greece in
the fifth century B.C. It seems more likely, however, that this
man is Astyages, the son of Cyrus the First of Persia. Astyages
may well be the man, who is called "Darius the Mede" in the
book of Daniel, who took the kingdom from Belshazzar on
the night of the great drunken orgy in the city of Babylon
when the handwriting of God appeared on the wall.

Sixty-five miles east of the city of Teheran, in the present
land of Iran, a great rock rises out of the plains in lonely
splendor. It crests some thirteen hundred feet above the
level of the plain. Five hundred feet up the side of the rock
a great area has been smoothed off which contains many
carved inscriptions and figures. The rock is called the Rock
of Behistun, and the inscriptions were carved there by the
Persian monarch, Darius the Great, who left a record of his
own kingdom and genealogy. His father was Cyrus the Great
and his grandfather was Astyages, also called Arsamanes. At
the time of the events of the book of Esther, Astyages would
have been a youth of about eighteen years of age, having but
recently ascended to the throne of Persia. The fact that the
Book of Esther never gives us the historic name of this

Ahasuerus doubtless indicates that this is not germane to the significance of the story, but it is interesting to see a possible connection to the Book of Daniel.

If we regard this story as a kind of mirror we shall see ourselves here. At the point the story opens, we find the kingdom lying at peace. The king is holding a feast which lasts for one hundred and eighty days, perhaps the longest feast ever known to man—six months long! Obviously there was no threat to this kingdom from the outside. It was a time of peace and blessing, fullness and fruitfulness. The king was perfectly free to do nothing but display the lavish glory of the riches of his kingdom.

We know from other scriptures that each man is made to be just such a king, ruling over such an empire. Our empire is our life, reaching out to touch all those with whom we come in contact and over whom we have influence. Our capital city, corresponding to Susa in the book of Esther, is our body. With its brain, heart, and nervous system, it is a marvelously complex and intricate mechanism. Through it, by means of the senses, reports from the empire without are brought to the king. From it, through the eyes and voice and hands, flow those responses that vitally affect the empire from one end to the other.

## More Than a Body

But everyone knows that man is more than a body. There is an invisible part which forms our personality, that immaterial but conscious part that lives with and expresses itself through the body. Even a baby realizes that man is more than an animated piece of beefsteak. Years ago I was lying in bed one morning when my three-year old daughter crawled into bed with me. I was trying to catch up on my beauty sleep (I need all of that I can get), and she was trying to wake me up. She pinched me and poked me, but I would not open my eyes. Finally, she reached up and pried open one of my eyelids. Leaning over to peer within, she said "Are you in there, daddy?" Thus she made it unmistakably clear that she knew man is more than a piece of meat with a nervous system!

This immaterial something that controls the life of the kingdom is represented here by the king. The Bible calls it the soul of man; it involves the faculties of mind, emotion, and will. The will, acted upon by the mind and the emotions, exercises authority within the kingdom. Whatever the king does affects the entire kingdom. Whatever occurs in your soul—the realm of your mind, your emotions, or your will—has an immediate effect, not only on the capital city of your body, but upon the empire—all those with whom you come in contact and over whom you have influence.

The Bible confirms the fact that man was made to be king. In Psalm 8, David acknowledges to God the place that God has given man:

Thou hast given him dominion over the works of thy hands;
    thou hast put all things under his feet,
all sheep and oxen,
    and also the beasts of the field,
the birds of the air, and the fish of the sea,
    whatever passes along the paths of the sea.

(Ps. 8:6–8)

God intended man to be a king, to have power and authority. But it was a derived authority; he was to manifest the glory of the invisible God. That is, he was to be the human vehicle of the divine life. As man gave himself to the task of properly governing the earth over which he was established as king, he would be displaying the majesty and glory of the God who indwelt him. Unfallen Adam, in the garden of Eden, was just such a king. Like Ahasuerus here, his whole empire lay at rest and he was free to do nothing more than manifest the riches and the fruitfulness and the glory of his kingdom, while enjoying unhindered communion with God.

But if man is made to commune with God there must be provision within man for that communion. There is, then, a function which lies below the level of the conscious life. It is this subconscious life which we call the human spirit. This spirit, designed to be the place of communion between the soul of man and the Holy Spirit of God, is pictured for us in the book of Esther by the queen, who, as the story opens, is Queen Vashti:

> And when these days were completed, the king gave for all the people present in Susa the capital, both great and small, a banquet lasting for seven days, in the court of the garden of the king's palace. There were white cotton curtains and blue hangings caught up with cords of fine linen and purple to silver rings and marble pillars, and also couches of gold and silver on a mosaic pavement of porphyry, marble, mother-of-pearl and precious stones. Drinks were served in golden goblets, goblets of different kinds, and the royal wine was lavished according to the bounty of the king. And drinking was according to the law, no one was compelled; for the king had given orders to all the officials of his palace to do as every man desired. Queen Vashti also gave a banquet for the women in the palace which belonged to King Ahasuerus. (Esther 1:5-9)

It is the presence of the human spirit within man which makes an immortal being—just as the whole hope of a continuing kingdom lies in the queen. When a king without a queen dies, the whole kingdom perishes—at least the dynasty does. So also, if man were nothing more than a body and a soul, then when man died he would die like an animal. Humanism insists that man is nothing more than an animal. He has a body and a soul as an animal does and, therefore, he can be treated like an animal. He can be bred like an animal and he can be improved like an animal, for he breathes like one, eats like one, and dies like one. But the Bible flatly contradicts this, and says that man is more than body and soul; he also has a spirit. It is the spirit of man which, the book of Ecclesiastes tells us, does not perish when the man dies, but "returns to God who gave it."

It is also in the realm of the spirit that man finds his comfort and counsel from a higher being. In the book of Esther, the queen provides this place of communion for the king. She is the one to whom the king goes for private fellowship and comfort. In the same way, what takes place between the soul and spirit of man is the most intimate, most essential activity of man's nature. So intimate and delicate is this union between the soul and the spirit (portrayed by the king and queen), that only one thing can expose it. In Hebrews 4:12 we read, "The word of God is living and active, sharper than any two-edged sword, piercing to the division of soul and spirit." Only the Word of God can make distinction between these two, revealing the innermost recesses of our life at the deepest level of existence.

So, as we move into the book of Esther, we have our key: the king is a picture of the soul of man, comprising mind, emotions, and will. His capital city, Susa, is the body, in which all his decisions and actions will be most immediately felt. His empire is the sphere of influence each man has in life. And finally, his queen is the spirit of man. It is so closely bound to his soul that no division or separation can be seen. The queen, bound in marriage to the king, depicts the place of fellowship, refreshment, and communion with God which is intimately related to our soul. Each of us is a walking book of Esther, and we shall see how accurate this portrayal is as the story progresses.

## Chapter 2

# A PAIR OF QUEENS

The great feast of King Ahasuerus began on a note of joy and merrymaking, but it did not end that way. Before the feast was over, a tragic action on the part of the king instantly severed his communion with his queen, and introduced a principle which was to destroy the peace of the entire kingdom:

> On the seventh day, when the heart of the king was merry with wine, he commanded . . . the seven eunuchs who served King Ahasuerus as chamberlains, to bring Queen Vashti before the king with her royal crown, in order to show the peoples and the princes her beauty; for she was fair to behold. But Queen Vashti refused to come at the king's command conveyed by the eunuchs. At this the king was enraged, and his anger burned within him. (Esther 1:10–12)

Here, in pictorial form, is the story of the fall of man. In the garden of Eden man was intended to display in his own human personality all the majesty, glory, wisdom, and might of the God who indwelt him. But here, the king is not content to display the authority that was properly his. As the party goes on he seems to feel that the glory and majesty are of his own making. Lifted up with pride and weakened by his own indulgence, he foolishly sends for the queen to come and display her beauty before the crowd. In a sense he is attempting to pervert his own nature, violating, by the use of his reason and will, the revelation available to him in the place of private and intimate communion.

Perhaps we can understand this scene better if we ask when it was that Adam actually fell? Did he fall when Eve ate of the forbidden fruit? No! That was when Eve fell—that was the fall of woman! But it was also the means by which the tempter gained access to the man. Adam fell when, confronted with the fact of his wife's disobedience, he deliberately chose to assert the supremacy of emotion (his love for his wife), over the revelation of his spirit wherein God spoke to him. When he thus violated the function of his spirit by asserting the supremacy of his soul, he became a fallen being. He tried to reverse the order of his nature to make his reason superior to revelation, and this has been the hallmark of fallen man ever since.

When the queen was summoned to appear before the king in this wrongful fashion, she refused to do so. Then, instead of honestly facing the rash pride that made him act so foolishly, the king summoned his counselors and angrily asked them what he should do with the reluctant queen. They slyly insinuated that the fault was all the queen's, and if he did not act to support his foolish demand he would encourage a revolt among the women of the kingdom and "there would be contempt and wrath in plenty." This was, of course, a lie, just as it was a lie when the tempter in the garden suggested to Eve that God was putting unwarranted restrictions upon her freedom, and if she didn't act to claim her fancied rights, she would never realize the full potential of her being and would be troubled with endless regrets.

## Unchangeable Law

As a result of this advice, King Ahasuerus made a choice from which he could not retreat. The evil counselors said to the king,

> "If it please the king, let a royal order go forth from him, and let it be written among the laws of the Persians and the Medes so that it may not be altered, that Vashti is to come no more before King Ahasuerus." (Esther 1:19)

This advice pleased the king, and letters were sent out to all the provinces in the entire domain of the empire to this effect. The law which the king thus promulgated was to be "written among the laws of the Persians and the Medes"— a law which could not be changed; the king himself must be forever subject to it.

In the greater parable of our own lives this unalterable law is known as "the law of sin and death." It is the law of retribution, or the law of inevitable consequence. When Adam was approached by Eve with the fruit of disobedience and he understood clearly what the issues were, he deliberately chose what his reason said over what God's revelation taught and ate of the fruit, thus cutting himself off from the glory of God in his own spirit. He chose the desire of his heart over fellowship with God, and set in motion a string of circumstances he was powerless to alter.

So the human spirit became dark and unresponsive and

man entered upon the lonely restlessness that has characterized him ever since. Man became a soulish being, governed
only by his mind, emotions, and will. His own ego, sitting on
the throne of his kingdom, brooking no opposition, is the
highest authority he knows. He has lost the joy and peace
and insights which were made available to him in the communion of his spirit with God's Spirit, and he is helpless to
reverse this fact. Here is ample explanation for all the folly,
injustice, evil, sin, misery, and darkness of human life as
we know it today.

Chapter 2 begins the story of redeeming grace. It opens
with the king vainly seeking to satisfy his restless soul in a
fruitless search for someone to fill the vacuum of his life:

> After these things, when the anger of King Ahasuerus
> had abated, he remembered Vashti and what she had
> done and what had been decreed against her. (Esther
> 2:1)

Man can never forget that he has a spirit. Though dark and
unresponsive to his present longings, it remains as a vestigial
memory of the joys and delights he was intended by God to
have. The king cannot be satisfied with the choice he has
made. His heart is empty; he is searching for someone, and
he is restless and unhappy.

### Driven by Loneliness

This is the whole story of human life without God. Dr.
Karl Jung, the great Austrian psychologist, says that man is
suffering from a neurosis of emptiness. He says, "When God
goes, goal goes; and when goal goes, purpose goes; and when

purpose goes, meaning goes; and when meaning goes, life goes dead on our hands." Man is forever restless and dissatisfied, never daring to be alone with his own thoughts, always demanding something to anesthetize the pain of his own loneliness. That yearning search is portrayed in this next section:

> Then the king's servants who attended him said, "Let beautiful young virgins be sought out for the king. And let the king appoint officers in all the provinces of his kingdom to gather all the beautiful young virgins to the harem in Susa the capital, under custody of Hegai the king's eunuch who is in charge of the women; let their ointments be given them. And let the maiden who pleases the king be queen instead of Vashti." This pleased the king, and he did so. (Esther 2:2-4)

Driven by loneliness man begins his aching search. But he little realizes what is involved, and the God who made man is unwilling to abandon him to the result of his own foolish choice. At this point in our story, therefore, we are introduced to two of the most important characters in the book:

> Now there was a Jew in Susa the capital whose name was Mordecai, the son of Jair, son of Shimei, son of Kish, a Benjaminite, who had been carried away from Jerusalem among the captives carried away with Jeconiah king of Judah, whom Nebuchadnezzar king of Babylon had carried away. He had brought up Hadassah, that is Esther, the daughter of his uncle, for she had neither father nor mother; the maiden was beautiful and lovely, and when her father and her mother died, Mordecai adopted her as his own daughter. (Esther 2:5-7)

As a Jew, Mordecai belongs to the nation chosen by God to be his point of contact with the human race. Jesus himself said, "Salvation is of the Jews." This strange race was chosen to be the instrument in the hands of the Holy Spirit by which the world was to be redeemed, and it was through Jesus, the Jew, that redemption was accomplished. Mordecai's name, "Little man," suggests the humility of the One who laid aside his glory and became man, to die at last upon a cross of shame that man might enter once again into life (Phil. 2:5–8). It is not difficult, therefore, to see in Mordecai the Spirit of Christ, the Holy Spirit, whose specific work is to restore man to the fellowship with God which he had lost.

Mordecai had a lovely young cousin whose name was Esther. In Hebrew her name is Hadassah, which means "Myrtle," a lowly shrub that was commonly regarded as the symbol of Israel. Her Persian name, Esther, is usually taken to mean "Star," but Gesenius, one of the greatest of Hebrew authorities, says that it is taken from the word "to hide." It means, therefore, "something hidden," and is beautifully descriptive of the spirit of man—so hidden in our essential nature that we can only describe it in terms of mystery such as "the super-ego," "the id," or "the subconscious."

Though Mordecai is really Esther's cousin, we read that after the death of her own father and mother, he adopted her as his own daughter. Thus the union between Esther and Mordecai is perfectly descriptive of the union of the human spirit with the Holy Spirit, accomplished by the process of adoption. Paul says in Romans 8:15: "You did not receive the spirit of slavery to fall back into fear, but you have received the spirit of sonship. When we cry, 'Abba! Father!' it is the Spirit himself bearing witness with our spirit that we are children of God." The work of the Spirit of God in any individual's life can only begin when that human spirit is introduced into the family of God by the sovereign adoption of the Holy Spirit.

What we have seen thus far takes place in our lives on the subconscious level. The Holy Spirit moves in sovereign power upon the heart; he chooses it and awakens within it a hunger for the family of God. But all this must now be brought up to the level of conscious knowledge. In the language of our story, the union of the redeemed spirit and the soul of man (the king) must now be openly manifested.

### The Search

Thus, the next step is for the king to discover the lovely Esther, although he is quite unaware that Mordecai is moving to bring the two face to face. The Bible urges man to "seek the Lord while he may be found" (Isa. 55:6), and reminds us that "he rewards those who seek him" (Heb. 11:6); but it also reveals that it is really the Holy Spirit who is doing the seeking, and when our search is ended, we are invariably astounded to discover that it was not we who found him, but he who found us. So, in this account of Esther, we have what may be the classic example of the old proverb, "He pursued her until she captured him." In the course of the king's search, maiden after maiden was brought before the king, but he rejected them all. At last, Esther's turn came:

When the turn came for Esther the daughter of Abihail the uncle of Mordecai, who had adopted her as his own daughter, to go in to the king, she asked for nothing except what Hegai the king's eunuch, who had charge of the women, advised. Now Esther found favor in the eyes of all who saw her. And when Esther was taken to King Ahasuerus into his royal palace in the tenth month, which is the month of Tebeth, in the seventh year of his reign, the king loved Esther more than all the women, and she found grace and favor in his sight more than all the virgins, so that he set the royal crown on her head and made her queen instead of Vashti. (Esther 2:15–17)

This hardly needs interpreting. We can call this the conversion of King Ahasuerus. Esther came before him without any of the artificial emollients to beauty which the other maidens had used. She stood before him in the loveliness of natural beauty; and when the king saw her, he immediately loved her and set the sign of royal authority upon her head. He recognized in this lovely girl the answer to his empty, restless life, and in setting the crown upon her head he entered at last into the joy and comfort of a life made complete.

There was an immediate effect throughout the whole empire:

Then the king gave a great banquet to all his princes and servants; it was Esther's banquet. He also granted a remission of taxes to the provinces, and gave gifts with royal liberality. (Esther 2:18)

There is a sense in which the king had no right to this girl. She belonged to a special race, a race forbidden by its own law to marry with another race; she was a Jewess. Yet here in this foreign land, by the sovereign overruling grace of God, she is brought before the king and when he finds her he knows that this is the one for whom his heart has longed. How beautifully representative this is of the fact that we have no right to the grace of God in our lives. The king, in his gratitude, immediately expresses his joy with a great banquet and new laws that reach out to the farthest limits of his empire. There is a lifting of the burden of taxation; there is a distribution of royal gifts with great liberality.

Did you discover, when you became a Christian, what Paul meant when he wrote, "If any one is in Christ, he is a new creation; the old has passed away, behold, the new has come" (2 Cor. 5:17)? Was there, in your life, a sense of the lifting of the burden of sin and an enjoyment of God's royal gifts such as you never had dreamed of before? We sing in the old hymn:

> Heaven above is softer blue,
> Earth around is sweeter green,
> Something lives in every hue,
> Christless eyes have never seen.*

This experience is possible to all. We may not understand all that happened on the day when, by faith in Jesus Christ, we received a spirit made alive by grace. But if it has occurred, we know there has been a wonderful change. We can never be the same again. Much must yet happen before the full value of that transaction is realized, but already there is new joy, new liberty, new richness.

---

* George Wade Robinson, "Loved with Everlasting Love."

Chapter 3

# THE STRUGGLE FOR
# CONTROL

The joy of a new Christian is delightful to see and even more delightful to experience, but it is forever set against the background of a bloody, fearsome cross. No Christian walks continually in the sunshine beneath blue skies. He must soon learn that joy and sorrow go hand in hand, that out of death comes life, and that only in the mystery of the cross is discovered the secret of joy. So, immediately after the marriage of Esther and Ahasuerus, there is recorded an incident of somber import:

When the virgins were gathered together the second time, Mordecai was sitting at the king's gate. Now Esther had not made known her kindred or her people, as Mordecai had charged her; for Esther obeyed Mordecai just as when she was brought up by him. And in those days, as Mordecai was sitting at the king's gate, Bigthan and Teresh, two of the king's eunuchs, who guarded the threshold, became angry and sought to lay hands on King Ahasuerus. And this came to the knowledge of Mordecai, and he told it to Queen Esther, and Esther told the king in the name of Mordecai.

When the affair was investigated and found to be so, the
men were both hanged on the gallows. And it was recorded
in the Book of the Chronicles in the presence of the king.
(Esther 2:19–23)

Here is the first hint of the existence of an evil force which
is at work to destroy the king, and in picture, to capture the
mind, emotions and will of man and pervert these to its own
use. Nothing more is said of this incident at the moment,
but later on in this book it becomes of transcending importance in effecting the complete deliverance of the king.

At the time it happens, however, the king knows nothing
of this event. Mordecai (who represents for us the Holy
Spirit) is sitting in the gate of the city as a judge, but has not
yet gained access to the palace (the place of control). Un-
known to the king, he discovers the plot against the king's
life, reports it, and the adversaries are taken out and publicly
"nailed to a tree." The rendering "hanged on the gallows"
is not literal, but is an interpretation. The literal Hebrew is
that they were impaled, or nailed to a tree.

### By Means of the Cross

The parallel of this in Christian experience is easily traced.
Long before we ever knew it ourselves, the Lord Jesus Christ
through the Eternal Spirit offered himself without spot to
God as a living sacrifice upon a cross. He had taken upon
himself the evil that was determined to destroy the soul of
man. Thus, we read in Colossians 2:13:

And you, who were dead in trespasses and the uncircumci-
sion of your flesh, God made alive together with him, having forgiven us all our trespasses, having canceled the bond

which stood against us with its legal demands; this he set aside, *nailing it to the cross*. He disarmed the principalities and powers and made a public example of them, triumphing over them in it [that is, in the cross]. (emphasis added)

The principle of a cross is thus introduced to us as the only means by which God deals with evil. We may be ignorant of this truth for long years, but we shall never find deliverance from the power of sin until we learn the full meaning of the historic cross. Thus the incident of Bigthan and Teresh, we are told, was recorded in a book to which the king had access. We, too, have such a book. God has recorded for our edification the tremendously fascinating story of the cross, and has revealed that by means of that cross he intends to deliver us from the sinister power which is at work to rob us of our blessing in Christ. The actual deliverance has already been accomplished. It is our knowledge of it by means of the book which will make it effectual in our experience.

Now, if Christianity were nothing more than becoming a Christian, that is, being saved so that we may go to heaven when we die, the book of Esther would end right here. But this is not the end; it is not even the beginning of the end; it is simply the end of the beginning. So far, the story has but set the stage for the deliverance which God intends to work in the life of the king, just as he intends to work a similar deliverance in the kingdom of your own heart. The experience of conversion has made us fit for heaven, but many of us may be many years yet away from heaven. What is to happen in between? Are we to struggle on as best we can until at last we are taken to be with the Lord? It is tragically true that many Christians know no more of the

Christian life than having their sins forgiven and waiting, often in heartbreak and defeat, for the time when God shall call them home.

But there is much more to come! We pick up the story in the opening of chapter 3:

> After these things King Ahasuerus promoted Haman the Agagite, the son of Hammedatha, and advanced him and set his seat above all the princes who were with him. And all the king's servants who were at the king's gate bowed down and did obeisance to Haman; for the king had so commanded concerning him. But Mordecai did not bow down or do obeisance. Then the king's servants who were at the king's gate said to Mordecai, "Why do you transgress the king's command?" And when they spoke to him day after day and he would not listen to them, they told Haman, in order to see whether Mordecai's words would avail; for he had told them that he was a Jew. And when Haman saw that Mordecai did not bow down or do obeisance to him, Haman was filled with fury. (Esther 3:1–5)

Mordecai we know, but who is Haman? He is suddenly introduced into the record here and an immediate antagonism develops between Mordecai and Haman. Haman is the prime minister of the kingdom, but Mordecai will not bow before him, though this is the command of the king. Who is this sinister figure?

We find a clue to the answer in the man's parentage. He is called "Haman, the son of Hammedatha, the Agagite." What is an Agagite? Here we will need to do a little detective work. If you haven't yet learned the thrill of studying our Bible as though you were a Perry Mason, you've missed a great deal. It is far more interesting than a murder mystery, for this concerns you! An Agagite is a descendant of Agag, and if we turn to a concordance we find there is an Agag in Scripture. In the days of Saul, the first king of Israel, the prophet Samuel was sent by God to order King Saul to destroy the Amalekites of whom Agag was the king. We have the account in 1 Samuel 15:

> And Samuel said to Saul, "The Lord sent me to anoint you king over his people Israel; now therefore hearken to the words of the Lord. Thus says the Lord of hosts, 'I will punish what Amalek did to Israel in opposing them on the way, when they came up out of Egypt. Now go and smite Amalek, and utterly destroy all that they have; do not spare them, but kill both man and woman, infant and suckling, ox and sheep, camel and ass.'" (1 Sam. 15:1-3)

Saul's commission was unmistakable! He was explicitly told to destroy all the Amalekites—to totally obliterate this people. This grisly command seems difficult to understand until we remember the incident recorded in the seventeenth chapter of Exodus when Israel was on its way through the wilderness from Egypt to Canaan. We are told there:

> Then came Amalek and fought with Israel at Rephidim. And Moses said to Joshua, "Choose for us men, and go out, fight with Amalek; tomorrow I will stand on the top of the hill with the rod of God in my hand." So Joshua did as Moses told him, and fought with Amalek; and Moses, Aaron, and Hur went up to the top of the hill. Whenever Moses held up his hand, Israel prevailed; and whenever he lowered his hand, Amalek prevailed. (Exod. 17:8-11)

The isssue of the battle did not lie in the fighting of Israel, but in the uplifting of the rod of God held in Moses' hand.

When Moses grew weary, Aaron and Hur stood on each side and held his hands until the battle was won. At the end of the battle the Lord said to Moses:

> "Write this as a memorial in a book and recite it in the ears of Joshua, that I will utterly blot out the remembrance of Amalek from under heaven. . . . The Lord will have war with Amalek from generation to generation." (Exod. 17: 14–16)

### The Principle of Evil

God has declared war with Amalek forever. He will never make peace with it. If we trace Amalek even further back, we discover that he was the grandson of Esau—the same Esau of whom God said, "Jacob have I loved but Esau have I hated." These Amalekites, descendants of Esau, are singled out in Scripture as a picture of the principle of evil at work in the human heart with which God will never make peace. Throughout Scripture, Amalek is always the enemy of all that God wants to do.

To return to the account in 1 Samuel, we read of Saul:

> And he took Agag the king of the Amalekites alive, and utterly destroyed all the people with the edge of the sword. But Saul and the people spared Agag, and the best of the sheep and of the oxen and of the fatlings, and the lambs, and all that was good, and would not utterly destroy them; all that was despised and worthless they utterly destroyed. (1 Sam. 15:8–9)

Saul, in his foolish ignorance, felt that he knew better than God. He spared Agag and thus presumed to find good in what God had declared to be bad. For this failure Samuel was sent to tell Saul that the kingdom was to be taken from him and given to another. Now, centuries later, here is Haman the Agagite, a representative of the tribe against whom God has declared war forever.

The New Testament reveals that there is in every life, even a Christian life, a satanic principle at work. It is called by various names—pride, sin, the flesh. It lives only to exalt itself, as we see depicted in Haman here. The man of the flesh is never so happy as when the world around him is bowing and scraping and doing obeisance to him. Pride loves to be flattered. Our egos seek to be bolstered constantly. Our pride is forever seeking status and position in the eyes of others. It glories in prestige and prominence.

But within the Christian, Haman has an implacable enemy —it is our Mordecai, the Holy Spirit. The New Testament says, "The desires of the flesh are against the Spirit, and the desires of the Spirit are against the flesh; for these are opposed to each other" (Gal. 5:17). There can never be peace between them, for God has said he will make war against Amalek from generation to generation. Thus we read in Romans 8: "The mind that is set on the flesh is hostile to God" (v. 7). No matter how fine and respectable the flesh may appear to us, it is inherently displeasing to God. It can never be made acceptable to him.

The Holy Spirit has gained a bridgehead in the Christian heart for one purpose only: that he might oppose this diabolical, satanic influence within us which so subtly and cleverly deceives and destroys us. He has come so that we might have deliverance from this traitorous "friend." But the presence of the Spirit in the heart arouses the flesh to an explosion of fury. Have you discovered that? When you first

became a Christian you may have felt that life should go on
smoothly and easily from then on; but it was not very long
before you discovered this was not the case. You found fight-
ings and frustrations within. You found yourself in the center
of a vast and swirling torment, an explosion of tension and
tumult.

As long as Haman is in the seat of power the whole kingdom will be affected by his evil designs, even the communion
of the king and the queen will be affected. There can be no
peace while Haman is controlling the throne. But the king
is not at all aware of his evil character. To him he appears as
a trusted and reliable friend. The problem, then, is how to
get the evil man out and the good man in. Since Haman
rules by the will of the king, it will be necessary to open the
king's eyes as to the true nature of his prime minister.

It is not an easy task, but the Holy Spirit has launched
upon nothing less than this as his goal in our lives. The
enemy is crafty and subtle and not easily dislodged, but until
he is overthrown the kingdom can never know peace. But
Haman knows that he cannot prevail if Mordecai ever gains
the king's ear. The battle is now joined. Who will prevail?

## Chapter 4

## THE CRAFTY FOE

Never underestimate the power of the enemy! That is a vital principle in military warfare and many a battle has been lost because that principle was ignored. It is important, therefore, that we understand the strategy of the flesh in its unending battle with the Spirit of God. Like the apostle Paul who had learned to live in victory over the enemy within, we must be able to say, "We are not ignorant of his devices." Having learned the character of Haman the Agagite, we are now told how he works.

Haman is determined to use the king to destroy Mordecai, but he does not launch a frontal attack against him. He is far too clever for that.

> But he disdained to lay hands on Mordecai alone. So, as they had made known to him the people of Mordecai, Haman sought to destroy all the Jews, the people of Mordecai, throughout the whole kingdom of Ahasuerus. (Esther 3:6)

As a Christian, how long would you entertain the thought of rejecting God's influence outright? In the first joy of Chris-

tian experience you would be repelled at any suggestion that
you tell the Holy Spirit to go to hell. The tempter never
starts there with us. He does not begin at the center where
he must ultimately come; he begins at the periphery of our
life, in the area of our attitudes rather than our convictions.
So Haman begins, not with Mordecai, but with the people
of Mordecai, the Jews. In the Bible, the story of the Jews is
the revelation of God at work among men. The whole purpose of this strange nation is that in their history we might
see unquestioned evidences of God at work. Therefore, in
the story, Mordecai's people, the Jews, represent that which
gives evidence to the world of God at work.

How do others around you know that God is at work in
your life? Will it be by what you say? Not necessarily—words
lose their meaning unless they are backed by deeds. Neither
will it be by religious activities, which can be nothing but
pious hypocrisy. But there are unmistakable signs. They are
listed in Galatians: "The fruit of the Spirit is love, joy, peace,
patience, kindness, faithfulness, gentleness, self-control" (Gal.
5:22–23).

Here are the true marks of God at work in a life. Shabby
imitations of these are possible for a while, but the true
qualities can never be produced apart from the supernatural
activity of the Holy Spirit. These are "the people of Mordecai" in your life as a Christian. It is here that the flesh within
begins its attack.

The whole strategy of the flesh is to convince us that these
attitudes are marks of weakness, that they are not really for
our good. We must, of course, always pay lip-service to them,
but when it comes to really wanting them in our life the
enemy seeks to convince us that we would get along much
better without them, that it is really the opposite attitudes

that will pay off for us. If we can be led to distrust and reject the attitudes of godliness, we will thereby frustrate the work of the Holy Spirit in our life.

## The Right Day for Evil

To accomplish this aim, Haman employs his favorite tactic —fear. In this particular case it is the form of fear we call superstition. All superstition is fear and fear is the enemy of faith. So, we read in verse 7:

> In the first month, which is the month of Nisan, in the twelfth year of King Ahasuerus, they cast Pur, that is the lot, before Haman day after day; and they cast it month after month till the twelfth month, which is the month of Adar. (Esther 3:7)

What a strange procedure! But the casting of lots to determine a lucky day on which to do something was common practice in oriental kingdoms. It is very similar to the practice today of shooting dice in order to select a propitious day for some activity. When the record says, "They cast it month after month till the twelfth month," it does not mean they shook dice for a whole year in front of Haman. It means that every cast made stood for a different day. A cast was made for each day of the calendar and if a propitious number turned up that day was regarded as a lucky day; thus they went through 365 casts before they found the lucky day. When they found it, it was in the twelfth month called the month of Adar.

This whole process made it possible for Haman to go to the king and say, "Look! If you really want good luck in your

life, if you want fortune to smile upon you, there's only one
thing to do—get rid of these people! I've read your horoscope
and on this one particular day if you will move against your
enemies you will discover that all the stars are working in
your favor. It is your weakness in letting these people live
that is causing the problems in your kingdom, and if you
want to break away from these limiting restrictions you must
obey the stars and all will be well."

Do you ever knock on wood whenever you speak of good
health or prosperity? Perhaps you smile lamely and make a
joke of it, but nevertheless, you feel that if you don't knock,
something bad may happen to you. Do you ever throw salt
over your shoulder, or refuse to walk under a ladder, or
avoid the number thirteen? Why do we do these superstitious
things? Is it not a lingering fear that some jealous spirit may
take away our prosperity or bring bad luck upon us? We are
afraid of the jealousy of God. The tempter has planted in
our hearts the feeling that God is not truly concerned about
our welfare, that we must take care of things ourselves. Our
fear makes us distrust the goodness of God.

Haman knows that if the king will heed this black magic,
he has succeeded in driving a wedge of distrust into his heart.
His first move is to make him distrust the people of Mordecai, to fear them and regard them as a threat rather than a
blessing. Just so the enemy within us makes us afraid to show
love and compassion; he labels these weakness and makes
us distrust them.

The wily prime minister couples with this awakening distrust an apparent solicitude for the king's welfare:

Then Haman said to King Ahasuerus, "There is a certain
people scattered abroad and dispersed among the peoples

in all the provinces of your kingdom; their laws are different from those of every other people, and they do not keep the king's laws, so that it is not for the king's profit to tolerate them. If it please the king, let it be decreed that they be destroyed, and I will pay ten thousand talents of silver into the hands of those who have charge of the king's business, that they may put it into the king's treasuries. (Esther 3: 8–9)

Talk to a king about a threat to his throne and you are touching something that is very close to his heart. When, in addition, you infer that you have a plan that will make him more wealthy than ever before, you interest him greatly. This is Haman's approach. He openly suggests that the people of Mordecai are not only unprofitable to him, but are a threat to his liberty, and that if he will remove them and trust Haman, Haman will make him rich.

Has Haman been talking to you recently? Has he suggested that it is not to your advantage to practice love, joy and peace, longsuffering, gentleness and meekness, but that if you live this way people will walk all over you? Has he, for instance, suggested that keeping your temper and giving a soft answer to those around you never really gets you anywhere, especially where you work, that it is the fellows who tell everyone off who get the promotions? Has he slyly insinuated that it is the man who is willing to stand up for his own rights and not let anyone walk all over him who gets advancement?

Has he, perhaps, whispered to you that honesty is really not the best policy, at least when it comes to filling out your income tax? After all, what the government won't know really won't hurt them, and you can save a lot of money by a few short cuts. Has he suggested that love is all right for

sentimentalists, but the only way to really defend the faith
and the American way of life is to picket those who don't
agree with you and hound them out of town?

Has Haman suggested that good manners and courteous
words are needed for business and for strangers, but at home
you can let your hair down and say what you like to your
wife and kids; they will respect you all the more for it? Has
he been talking to you? Does it sound pretty good? Does it
sound like it will work, especially when he can show you
from your horoscope that this is the day to throw your weight
around?

Well, then, look at the program of defeat that inevitably
follows. It begins with the fateful decision of the king:

> So the king took his signet ring from his hand and gave it
> to Haman the Agagite, the son of Hammedatha, the enemy
> of the Jews. And the king said to Haman, "The money is
> given to you, the people also, to do with them as it seems
> good to you." (Esther 3:10–11)

### Who Is in Control?

Nothing can be done in your life without the consent of
your will. You cannot pass the buck to someone else. You
alone must bear final responsibility for what happens, for
nothing can be done either good or evil apart from the
consent of your will. You may be perfectly sincere and confident that you are doing the right thing, as this king was,
but sincerity is never any defense against error. If evil gains
control of your life it is because you have permitted it to
do so.

Furthermore, it is clear from this that when we make a

decision we hand the authority to act to another. The New Testament declares that man can do nothing by himself. We are not made to be activists; we are made only to be deciders. As Paul reminds us in Romans 6, we are either instruments of righteousness or unrighteousness; in either case we are merely the instruments. The power to act belongs to another. The tragedy of evil choices is that when we commit ourselves to such forces within us they often act far beyond our desires. Nevertheless, the decision to permit them to act is ours alone.

This decision on the part of the king is immediately followed by a widespread disturbance:

> Then the king's secretaries were summoned on the thirteenth day of the first month, and an edict, according to all that Haman commanded, was written to the king's satraps and to the governors over all the provinces and to the princes of all the peoples, to every province in its own script and every people in its own language; it was written in the name of King Ahasuerus and sealed with the king's ring. Letters were sent by couriers to all the king's provinces, to destroy, to slay, and annihilate all Jews, young and old, women and children, in one day, the thirteenth day of the twelfth month, which is the month of Adar, and to plunder their goods. A copy of the document was to be issued as a decree in every province by proclamation to all the peoples to be ready for that day. The couriers went in haste by order of the king, and the decree was issued in Susa the capital. (Esther 3:12–15)

The whole of the kingdom is immediately involved in whatever the king does. The effect of this decision was felt throughout the entire empire. What we do is never done in a corner. What we decide in the depths of our heart affects everyone who knows us. The decision made in the innermost part of our thoughts sooner or later touches the lives of everyone with whom we have to do. Secret thoughts must ultimately become evident in deeds. We cannot give ourselves to playing with thoughts in secret that do not sooner or later break out in actual deeds. Thus disturbance is always the result of some inner decision.

The final step in the program of defeat initiated by the flesh is one of delusion: "And the king and Haman sat down to drink; but the city of Susa was perplexed" (v. 15). The king is quite confident that he has taken a wise step, but he is totally deluded. He thinks he is acting in his own interest. He is grateful to Haman for his obvious concern for his welfare so he invites him in to celebrate with a glass or two of wine. But outside in the city there is nothing but confusion and perplexity. No one knows what to do; this strange edict has thrown them into confusion.

Have you ever had a drinking session with yourself to congratulate yourself for the clever way you solved a problem in your life? You've had to cut corners a bit and maybe tell off a few people along the way, but you got what you wanted. It's a pretty good feeling, isn't it? You go home and pat yourself on the back and congratulate yourself. You and Haman have a drinking session together. But when you get around to taking the next step you discover you don't know what to do. You've lost your sense of direction. You started out well, but before you know it somehow you have become confused and distracted. Trivial things have become all-important and that which is of vital importance you treat as though it were of no concern.

Is this where you are living today? Are you a victim of

your own sense of dedication? You meant to do right, you tried to do right, you thought you were making the right choices on the basis of what was the right thing to do, but it has turned out to be so confusing, so baffling! Many Christians live right here, defeated, deluded, disappointed, and they don't know why. The Lord Jesus said, "If your eye is sound, your whole body will be full of light; but if . . . the light in you is darkness, how great is the darkness!" (Matt. 6:22–23)

Such darkness in Christian lives is what the Scriptures call the reign of sin. The king (your will) is wholly under the influence of the evil prime minister. The result in the kingdom is perplexity, confusion, despair, and darkness. The king never meant it to be so, but at long as he is unaware of the true nature of Haman he is helpless to correct this condition. His deliverance and that of the empire's can only begin when he is made to see the true character of Haman.

At this point, Mordecai begins to act. In his action we shall learn the full meaning of the great statement in Galatians: "The Spirit lusts against the flesh so that you cannot do the thing that you would." All hope for deliverance from the subtle flesh lies in that sovereign activity of the Spirit of God.

## Chapter 5

## DIVINE GRIEF

When the confusion and perplexity that result from Haman's fiendish proposal to the king are felt throughout the capital city, Mordecai's reaction is profound and significant:

> When Mordecai learned all that had been done, Mordecai rent his clothes and put on sackcloth and ashes, and went out into the midst of the city, wailing with a loud and bitter cry; he went up to the entrance of the king's gate, for no one might enter the king's gate clothed with sackcloth. And in every province, wherever the king's command and his decree came, there was great mourning among the Jews, with fasting and weeping and lamenting, and most of them lay in sackcloth and ashes. (Esther 4:1–3)

What a picture of grief! The Jews are thrown into a panic by the hideous pronouncement and express their sorrow by weeping and lamenting and wearing sackcloth and ashes. But it is Mordecai alone who fully understands the true import of the situation. He knows that not only will this destroy the people of God throughout the whole kingdom, but it will touch the very throne. The queen herself, as a Jewess, is in danger, for the decree had become the law of the Medes and the Persians and it could not be changed. Therefore he, too, reacted with bitter and painful grief.

Lay this parable from the Old Testament alongside a passage from the New. In Ephesians 4:30 the apostle Paul warns us, "Do not grieve the Holy Spirit of God, in whom you were sealed for the day of redemption." What is it that grieves the Holy Spirit? The next verse tells us, "Let all bitterness and wrath and anger and clamor and slander be put away from you, with all malice." These are the things that grieve the Spirit. They are the works of the flesh, the exact opposites of the fruit of the Spirit—love, joy, peace, long-suffering, gentleness, goodness, etc.

It is most remarkable to see that what grieves the heart of God is not the enmity of the sinner so much as the unthinking foolishness of the saint. The problem we face in the book of Esther is not that of stubborn, deliberate opposition to the will of God. When we manifest that attitude, God simply lets us go ahead and live out our folly, for we can only learn to reject our stubborn pride by experiencing something of the sad results that follow. But these times of deliberate rebellion are not nearly as frequent as the occasions when, wanting to do right and thinking we are doing right, we fall into a circumstance or reaction which ultimately proves very wrong and destroys the fruit of the Spirit in our lives. Thus sincerely, with the best of intentions, quite openly and honestly, we launch upon a course which threatens ultimately to destroy our peace, our joy, our patience, our kindness, or our self-control. When this occurs we don't know what is wrong. We are confused and baffled.

### Self-Destruction

It is at such times that the Spirit of God is deeply grieved within us. Mordecai wept out of sympathy for the king and the kingdom because of the sorrow they unwittingly brought upon themselves. As a Jew he knew the history of his race. He knew that the Jews were under special protection from God wherever they went. He knew that no nation laid its hand upon the Jew in anger or in punishment with inpunity. This, incidentally, is the thing that Hitler forgot. Mordecai knew that if the king carried out his foolish intention to destroy these people, there would be an opposite reaction upon the kingdom; every nation that has ever touched the Jew in anger has itself been destroyed.

So also in the parable of our own lives, the Spirit knows that when we unthinkingly permit our natural human reactions to control us, we ultimately destroy ourselves in the process. Unrealized by us, this "natural reaction" creates in us tensions and pressures that result in neuroses and compulsions which tear us apart, causing us to come unglued in moments of pressure and creating depression of mind and spirit. This depression is what is referred to in Romans 6 as death: "The wages of sin is death." Death, there, does not mean the end of natural life. It means the absence of spiritual blessing—that is, barrenness, emptiness, a sense of futility and frustration. The Spirit within weeps out of sympathy and grief.

You see this spirit of grief in the Lord Jesus on his way to the tomb of Lazarus, leading a sorrowing, wailing company along the way. He knew that in a few moments he would speak the words that would bring that man who had been dead four days back to life, and all the grief and sorrow would be turned into joy. Yet we read that as he went to the tomb his spirit was deeply moved within him. The Greek is much stronger than the English. It says he was torn inside. Thus we have the shortest verse in our English Bible, "Jesus wept." The tears rolled down his face even in expectation of that moment of triumph and deliverance, because he knew the sorrow, heartache, and pain that inevitably result from human sin no matter what the final outcome might be.

Thank God for the grieving of the Spirit. It is this grieving Spirit within us that is the guarantee of God that he will never leave us in our ignorant folly. It marks the unwillingness of God to let us go stumbling along into the full results of our own wrong choices.

## Distress Signal

As yet, neither the king nor the queen is aware of Mordecai's grieved heart. Mordecai's only channel of approach to the king is through the queen and therefore it is imperative that she understand the whole situation. Thus we are next shown the results in the human spirit when the grieving of the Holy Spirit is made known:

> When Esther's maids and her eunuchs came and told her, the queen was deeply distressed; she sent garments to clothe Mordecai, so that he might take off his sackcloth, but he would not accept them. (Esther 4:4)

Do you recognize this? Here is the first uneasy realization that something is wrong. It does not take place in the soul at the level of the conscious life, but deep in the subconscious, in the depths of the spirit. Have you ever sensed that

you are living with a grieved Spirit? You don't know specifically yet what it is, but deep in your heart, you feel there is
something wrong. Perhaps, as here, you try to cover up your
disquiet by assuming a forced attitude of cheerfulness and
well-being. But the Holy Spirit is not so easily put off. You
find you cannot talk yourself out of your distress. Something
is wrong!

Esther immediately does the wise and sensible thing:

> Then Esther called for Hathach, one of the king's eunuchs,
> who had been appointed to attend her, and ordered him to
> go to Mordecai to learn what this was and why it was. (Es-
> ther 4:5)

There is never need to be in doubt as to exactly what may be
causing confusion and perplexity in our lives. The Spirit of
God is always willing to tell us exactly what is wrong if we
will seek as specifically and definitely as Esther does here.

But a word of warning may be in order. We need to carefully distinguish between the condemning voice of Satan
and the true grief of the Holy Spirit. The one is vague, un-
specific, creating a hazy sense of guilt, designed to trap us
into some legality or busy activity in the flesh. We have all
experienced that nagging feeling of undefined guilt which,
no matter how often we may ask about it, remains always
the same. We may be sure that it is the voice of Satan. It is
his attempt to get us concerned with our inner self so that
we will compensate in some other direction by assuming
some legal bondage or getting busy in a flurry of religious
activity. Satan well knows that if he can get us operating out
of the flesh we are utterly useless in the kingdom of God.

But on the other hand, the voice of the Spirit is always

specific and to the point—patiently, quietly insistent. If we refuse to allow the matter to come into our conscious thinking, he keeps continually bringing us back to it. We may not want to look at it and may try to shove it out of our mind, but we cannot escape the sense that something is wrong. If we will definitely and honestly go to him directly, we shall find it will immediately lead to a further clear revelation.

> Hathach went out to Mordecai in the open square of the city in front of the king's gate, and Mordecai told him all that had happened to him, and the exact sum of money that Haman had promised to pay into the king's treasuries for the destruction of the Jews. Mordecai also gave him a copy of the written decree issued in Susa for their destruction, that he might show it to Esther and explain it to her and charge her to go to the king to make supplication to him and entreat him for her people. And Hathach went and told Esther what Mordecai had said. (Esther 4:6–9)

Notice how clear and specific this is. Mordecai knew the whole story. He knew the exact sum of money that Haman, in secret, had told the king he would put into his treasury; he also had a copy of the decree. He revealed the whole plan to Esther in specific, exact detail.

It is also significant that the name of the servant who acted as an intermediary is Hathach, which means "the truth." When you realize that something has come between you and the Lord, some shadow has come in and hidden his face, where do you go to find out what it is? Have you not frequently found the answer in the Word of Truth? Perhaps in your morning devotional time, seeking light from the Scriptures, you found the Spirit of God illuminating a verse and making it speak out to you, and suddenly you knew the thing that was wrong. Or perhaps in prayer you asked God to make the matter clear and there came into your mind an image of something that was out of line and you could not shake it off. Out of the blue there comes a remembrance of that business deal you maneuvered, the word you spoke, or the thing you did, and you knew this was it—the truth! Perhaps a word of counsel or reproof comes from someone else and you know as he speaks that the thing he is saying is the truth. It is in some such way that the Spirit undertakes to make the whole matter clear to us.

### Reluctant to Die

Does it surprise us to see that when Esther understands the matter clearly her reaction is one of reluctance?

> Then Esther spoke to Hathach and gave him a message for Mordecai, saying, "All the king's servants and the people of the king's provinces know that if any man or woman goes to the king inside the inner court without being called, there is but one law; all alike are to be put to death, except the one to whom the king holds out the golden scepter that he may live. And I have not been called to come in to the king these thirty days." And they told Mordecai what Esther had said. (Esther 4:10–12)

What a remarkable picture this gives of the inner workings of our hearts. The king, you remember, is the soul—your mind, emotions, and will. The soul is a creature of moods and tends to reject unpleasant information when it is in a bad mood. Frequently we allow thoughts to live unexamined in our subconscious until such a time as we are in a good mood and are willing to think openly and seriously about them. Psychologists tell us this tendency explains the nature of many of our dreams. In a dream, we are sometimes confronted with thoughts that our conscious mind has resisted and refused to face. We are often reluctant to read or listen to anything that would tear the veil off the true nature of the flesh within us, but the Holy Spirit knows how to proceed.

At this point Mordecai acts with vigor and insistence. He sends word back to Esther immediately:

> Then Mordecai told them to return answer to Esther, "Think not that in the king's palace you will escape any more than all the other Jews. For if you keep silence at such a time as this, relief and deliverance will rise for the Jews from another quarter, but you and your father's house will perish. And who knows whether you have not come to the kingdom for such a time as this?" (Esther 4:13–14)

Mordecai is absolutely inflexible at this point. He will not let Esther delay or try to seek another way. He is saying: "Although you may not act, deliverance for the Jews will arise from another quarter." The idea is that God has an infinite number of ways to accomplish his will. We may fail in what he gives us to do, but that doesn't stop him from doing his will. God is never hindered by man's failure. But we may miss out on the beauty of God's perfection for us; we may "suffer loss," as Paul puts it.

Esther's reluctance to face the possibility of death is understandable, but there is no other way out. Like her, we may long seek to delay action on the painful matter of condemning the "natural" urges that rise within us, but there is no other way. "Unless a grain of wheat fall into the ground and

dies, it remains alone" (John 12:24). If we seek to control
the flesh by will power or discipline, we shall find it too
strong for us. It is no light thing to believe what Romans
tells us: we are crucified with Christ. It will mean we shall
have to face up squarely to the nauseous character of the
flesh within us and condemn it in its totality. We can no
longer defend any part of it or excuse it. Our will must be
squarely confronted with the whole issue and an irrevocable
commitment made.

The importance of this decision is highlighted by Mordecai's words to Esther: "Who knows whether you have not
come to the kingdom for such a time as this?" What is the
real purpose of conversion? Is it only that God might take
you to heaven some day? Is it that you might reign with him
in glory in the sweet by-and-by? No! "Thou art come to the
kingdom for such a time as *this.*" The Holy Spirit has entered
your life in order that you might live in fruitfulness and
victory right now, right where you live and work, that in
the day-to-day experiences of your life you might manifest the
fullness of the character of God. Your conversion is but the
beginning. It will never have any meaning unless you learn
to walk in victory over bitterness, resentment, malice, anger,
lust, anxiety, and every other manifestation of the flesh, *right
now!*

If we refuse to face up to this fact, if we try to make peace
with the flesh so as to avoid accepting the full meaning of
the death of Christ for us, we have no choice but to go on
under the dominion and reign of sin. Heaven may still be
ours at the end because of the work of Jesus Christ on our
behalf, but we shall look back upon a wasted and ruined life.
If this happens it will be our own fault, for the Holy Spirit
has entered our lives "for such a time as this."

## Righteous Fatalism

Esther is most impressed with the firm insistence of Mordecai at this point. The issue is now perfectly clear and she sends back to Mordecai a most significant answer:

> "Go, gather all the Jews to be found in Susa, and hold a fast on my behalf, and neither eat nor drink for three days, night or day. I and my maids will also fast as you do. Then I will go to the king, though it is against the law; and if I perish, I perish." Mordecai then went away and did everything as Esther had ordered him. (Esther 4:16–17)

With courage and grace, Esther bows to the will of Mordecai. In the symbolism of a fast she indicates her complete willingness to enter into death—a death three days and three nights long! Jesus said, "As Jonah was three days and three nights in the belly of the whale, so will the Son of Man be three days and three nights in the heart of the earth" (Matt. 12:40). Esther is saying in effect, "With the meaning of the death of Jesus Christ before me and the consciousness of what it will effect, I am willing to die myself—'If I perish, I perish'." Just as we must be willing to accept in practical experience the judgment of the cross upon our natural, Adamic life, so she was willing to enter into death.

If you laid the book of Romans alongside the book of Esther at this point, you would find yourself standing right at Romans 6:6: "We know that our old self was crucified with him so that the sinful body might be destroyed, and we might no longer be enslaved to sin." In this wonderful, typical way, the book of Esther is teaching us that the death of Jesus Christ actually involved the death of our old self with him; therefore we are no longer to operate on the basis of the flesh. Without reservation, it is declared to be absolutely worthless. When we believe that, then we can begin to walk in the liberty and freedom God has intended for us.

How beautifully Esther's words picture this identification of the believer with the death of Jesus Christ. This is not yet the realm of the soul, the emotional life, the feelings which are subject to change. Rather, this concerns the realm of the spirit, the deepest part of man's nature. What this declares is that down at the very deepest level of your life a fact has taken place from which all deliverance will stem. It means that if this has occurred, whether or not you feel like a Christian, you still are a Christian. Christ's death for you and your death with him are unchangeable facts, and nothing you do or don't do can affect them.

This is a truth we greatly need, for until we begin to believe what God says is true about what happened to us when Jesus Christ died, we will never have the confidence to accept the deliverance that he has based upon that truth. If you once died with him you are not the same—you never will be the same again. Even though temporarily you do fall into sinful acts which are the same as those you committed before you were a Christian, still you are not the same—you cannot be. You have been transferred, the New Testament says, "from the dominion of darkness . . . to the kingdom of his beloved Son" (Col. 1:13), and the evil one cannot lay his hands upon you any longer. You are not in bondage; you are a believer and your deliverance rests upon an unchangeable fact.

A number of years ago, I was talking with a young man who had been staying away from church for some time. When I asked him why, he said, "Well, I hesitate to come any longer because when I'm at work I can't seem to live like I ought to. There is so much failure in my life at work. I lose my temper and sometimes curse and say things that I shouldn't. That's why I don't want to come to church, because I feel like a hypocrite when I do."

I said, "You know, a hypocrite is someone who acts like something he isn't. When do you act that way?" "Well," he said, "if I came to church after the way I lived through the week, I'd be a hypocrite, wouldn't I?" I said, "Are you a Christian?" He said, "Yes, I am." "All right," I said, "if you are a Christian, then when is it that you do not act like one? At church or at work?" "Oh," he said, "I see what you mean. I'm being a hypocrite at work!" "Yes," I said, "when you come to church you're being what you really are for perhaps the first time that week."

It is not hypocritical to come among the people of God with a sense of weakness and even failure. You belong there —that's what Christians are. You may be a hypocrite at work, and if you wish to avoid acting like a hypocrite, that is the place to do it.

The point is this: You need not go on being deluded and deceived, because God has arranged a way out to the believer in Christ. "No temptation has overtaken you that is not common to man. God is faithful. . . ." Whether you are or not is beside the point. God's Word never changes. The death of Jesus Christ is an unchangeable fact in your experience if you have received him. "God is faithful, and he will not let you be tempted beyond your strength, but with the temptation will also provide the way of escape, that you may be able to endure it" (1 Cor. 10:13). He will bring you through if you rest upon the unchangeable fact of what he has already done in your life.

From this vantage point, the identification of the believer with the death of Jesus Christ, the Holy Spirit is ready to move into the realm of the conscious life, the soul (our emotions, reason, and will). It is necessary to bring to our conscious attention what is going on deep in our life before we can be delivered. And the power with which God works in our life will always be the power of a resurrected life.

So Esther, in grace and loveliness and on the third day, takes her courage in her hand and goes before the king. The fateful decision must now be his.

# Chapter 6

# THE DINNER THAT
# DELAYS

Esther is now standing outside the palace door, afraid to enter, wondering if the king will receive her or not. It is a moment of high drama. We pick up the story from chapter 5 of the text:

> On the third day Esther put on her royal robes and stood in the inner court of the king's palace, opposite the king's hall. The king was sitting on his royal throne inside the palace opposite the entrance to the palace; and when the king saw Queen Esther standing in the court, she found favor in his sight and he held out to Esther the golden scepter that was in his hand. Then Esther approached and touched the top of the scepter. And the king said to her, "What is it, Queen Esther? What is your request? It shall be given you, even to the half of my kingdom." (Esther 5:1-3)

The queen dressed in her royal robes of authority and power, comes to the king on the third day! In Scripture, the third day is always the day of resurrection. For three days and nights she has fasted as though she were dead, but now, in a sense risen from the dead, she comes to the king to make her request.

We have already learned that the human spirit, made alive in resurrection power by the indwelling of the Holy Spirit, becomes the means by which the Holy Spirit seeks to influence and repossess our minds, emotions, and will. Guidance imparted by the human spirit is therefore true, realistic, and morally upright because the human spirit is under the control of the Holy Spirit. This is why the translators of Scripture sometimes have great difficulty distinguishing between the human spirit and the Holy Spirit. In some versions of the Bible, the word "spirit" is spelled with a small *s* while in other versions it will be spelled in the same place with a capital *S*, simply because it is difficult to tell whether the writer means the Holy Spirit or the human spirit. But it really makes little difference since, in the redeemed spirit, the Holy Spirit is always in full control. It is the soul that is in rebellion, never the spirit.

That soul, the king, has the power to reject the pleadings of the spirit. The will must always give its consent to whatever occurs in our lives. This is why God moves to bring to our intelligent understanding the facts of the cross and resurrection that we may either accept their full implications or else deny them.

Even babies sense the supremacy of the will. A three-year-old can rule as a queen in a household. If you hold out your arms to her to hold her, she will sometimes look at you with icy disdain. If she decides to accept your offer, she regally holds out one arm like a scepter, and you know you are accepted. But if she is not in the mood she turns her head away, and there is nothing left to do but slink off and wait for a more opportune time. This is the power of the will.

We instinctively know we have a right to choose. Our soul was designed by God to this very end. God himself does not coerce the human will, but woos it and wins its consent.

Thus when God moves to bring to our intelligent understanding the facts of the cross and the resurrection, he does so in the fullness and beauty of resurrection power. Christ does not come to threaten us or berate us, but to overwhelm us with his loveliness. He lets us see him in the freshness and fragrance of his total adequacy and, melted by grace, we are ready to say, "Lord Jesus, whatever you want—anything you say—whatever you want me to do, I am ready to do."

Thus, on the third day Esther appears before the king, and he is greatly struck by her beauty. He is immediately ready to grant her request.

But now we read of something very strange:

And Esther said, "If it please the king, let the king and Haman come this day to a dinner that I have prepared for the king." Then said the king, "Bring Haman quickly, that we may do as Esther desires." So the king and Haman came to the dinner that Esther had prepared. And as they were drinking wine, the king said to Esther, "What is your petition? It shall be granted you. And what is your request? Even to the half of my kingdom, it shall be fulfilled." But Esther said, "My petition and my request is: If I have found favor in the sight of the king, and if it please the king to grant my petition and fulfil my request, let the king and Haman come tomorrow to the dinner which I will prepare for them, and tomorrow I will do as the king has said." (Esther 5:4–8)

Why this strange delay? Why should Esther put off making her request like this? The king seems quite eager to grant her desire—even to the half of his kingdom. Under the law of the Medes and Persians, this was the utmost a king was permitted to give away. Why then, this strange delay?

Have you ever experienced this in your relationship with the Lord? Have you ever come to the place where, captivated by the beauty of Christ and sensing something of the glory and joy he brings, you have, with complete sincerity and honesty, dedicated yourself anew to him? Perhaps you have gone forward in a meeting, or raised your hand, or knelt in the secrecy of your own room and given yourself again to Christ. Then you waited for God to act, and nothing happened. He seemed to do nothing about it. Perhaps you dedicated yourself to go to the mission field, or to enter a new line of endeavor. And then nothing happens—no doors open. You ask, "Why the delay? I've yielded, I'm ready, here am I, Lord, send me!" But nothing is done. How do you explain it?

### Time to Think

There are two reasons suggested in this account. The first is that God is never content with a decision that is based on emotions alone. We need to recognize this. We have seen that Haman can move the king as easily as Esther can. If decisions are to be based on emotions only they will continuously shift back and forth whichever way the wind blows. This is precisely the story of many Christians. But God is not content with this. So when a moment of surrender or dedication occurs, God frequently delays action in order to give us time to think the matter through and allow our understanding to catch up with our faith.

When I was still a young, growing Christian, I wanted to

be a surgeon. Even as a little boy in the early grades of school I would sit at my desk and manipulate my fingers so my knuckles would be supple enough to tie knots. I haunted every hospital I could get to and read everything I could on medicine. I learned the parts of the body, the nerves and the muscles, while still in high school.

Then quietly, I don't know quite how or when, I began to realize that God was moving in a different direction, and that he was suggesting to me that I consider entering the ministry. At first I resented this, and fought against it, resisting the insistent plea of the Spirit. But when the Spirit is after someone, he never gives up. Finally, in a moment of surrender and dedication, overwhelmed with the joy of what Christ meant to me, in my own room alone, I said to him, "All right, Lord, I'll be a minister, if that is what you want."

But then nothing happened! I expected an invitation the next day to preach at some prominent church, but it never came. I waited, and went on, doing the things that were before me to do. When I left the city of Chicago I went to Denver and from there, after a year or so, I went to Honolulu, after the war began. While the war was on, I was engaged in teaching Bible classes in bomb shelters, but still nothing was moving, no doors opened. It wasn't until the war ended, and I was discharged from the service, that the Lord opened the door for me to go to seminary and enter into training for the ministry. But I discovered that when I did go, when the door did open, I was much more ready for it. I realized so much more of what was involved in the ministry and felt that I was able to appropriate much more of the value of seminary because I knew what the battle was about.

So God knows the king needs time to base his decision on more than the warmth of his love alone. He needs to

understand certain facts, and in the next chapter we will see
how those facts are made clear to him. This all points up
the essential truth that all growth in grace requires that emotion must lead on to knowledge. Faith leads out first, but if
our understanding doesn't catch up, faith soon begins to fail.
"You will *know* the truth, and the truth will make you free"
(John 8:32, emphasis added).

### The Enemy Unmasked

A second reason for this delay on the part of Esther appears in the next section:

> And Haman went out that day joyful and glad of heart. But
> when Haman saw Mordecai in the king's gate, that he
> neither rose nor trembled before him, he was filled with
> wrath against Mordecai. Nevertheless Haman restrained
> himself, and went home; and he sent and fetched his friends
> and his wife Zeresh. And Haman recounted to them the
> splendor of his riches, the number of his sons, all the promo-
> tions with which the king had honored him, and how he
> had advanced him above the princes and the servants of the
> king. And Haman added, "Even Queen Esther let no one
> come with the king to the banquet she prepared but myself.
> And tomorrow also I am invited by her together with the
> king. Yet all this does me no good, so long as I see Mordecai
> the Jew sitting at the king's gate." Then his wife Zeresh and
> all his friends said to him, "Let a gallows fifty cubits high
> be made, and in the morning tell the king to have Mordecai
> hanged upon it; then go merrily with the king to the din-
> ner." This counsel pleased Haman, and he had the gallows
> made. (Esther 5:9–14)

The flesh is cunning and crafty in its subtlety, but the Holy
Spirit is more than a match for it. By these tactics of delay

and with amazing skill, the Holy Spirit tricks the flesh within us into an open display of pride and arrogance that shocks us, catches us up short, and makes us realize what is the true condition of our hearts. Delay gives opportunity for the flesh to grow puffed up with a sense of its own importance and thus to drop its subtlety and act in such open arrogance that even we can see how rotten and evil it is. Then we shall begin to judge it as an enemy rather than a friend.

Haman goes out to Esther's dinner walking on air. It looks to him as though he has won both the king and queen to his side. At first he is jubilant, but one thing sticks in his craw—outside the gate he sees Mordecai who refuses to bow and scrape before him. All the self-inflated joy he felt over the apparent favor shown him by Queen Esther is spoiled by this continual fly in his ointment. He seeks to relieve his wounded ego in the only way the flesh knows—by an orgy of self-praise. "And Haman recounted to them the splendor of his riches, the number of his sons, all the promotions with which the king had honored him, and how he had advanced him above the princes and the servants of the king."

There is nothing that soothes our battered egos more than sympathetic listeners to the tale of our own prowess. Have you ever indulged in this: "I said to him . . . and he said to me . . . and I said back to him . . . and I really told him . . ." and so on? Whatever comes from the Haman-nature within us is characterized by pride, and pride always blinds. When men become blind they are helpless and stumble unwittingly into folly. When I give way to pride and allow Haman to rule my life, I, too, become blind and stumble into some stupid, foolish action to my own detriment. I am tricked into some egotistical action or word. I become vain, arrogant, swaggering—and vulnerable! The kindest thing God can do, therefore, is to allow me to be-

come so puffed up in pride that I act in a way that shocks
me. Then I see the truth and give serious attention to the
program he has designed to deal with this.

In the Gospel accounts, the Lord Jesus is continually
stripping false pretenses from men and showing them exactly
what they are. Read the stories of his dealings with the
Pharisees and you will see this repeated pattern all the way
through. Men would come to him with questions obviously
contrived and designed to trap him and show him in the
wrong. Each question would be carefully worded to antici-
pate all possible answers that would make the questioner
look bad. Again and again he would allow them to state their
case, crawl out on a limb, and then his answer would be so
unexpected, so keenly perceptive, that he would leave them
chagrined, all their deceitfulness exposed, naked before the
eyes of the crowd. They hated him for it! They would gather
in little groups to whisper and plot his death. Our Lord
knew this was going on, and the whole story of the gospels
is that of how he continually exposed them and drove them
to the place where they did the deed—his crucifixion—which
ultimately revealed them for what they were before the whole
world.

So it is with Haman here: "Yet all this does me no good,"
he says, "so long as I see Mordecai the Jew sitting at the
king's gate." Then his wife Zeresh and his friends said to
him, "There is only one thing you can do. If something
stands in the way of self-expression and your need to satisfy
your own ego, then get rid of it—hang it! Let a gallows fifty
cubits high be made and tell the king to hang Mordecai on
that and then go merrily to dinner." As we have already seen,
the word "gallows" does not suggest a hangman's noose;
rather it is a tall pole on which a man is to be nailed or

impaled. It is, in effect, a cross. This is God's revelation to us that there is in each of us an element which would willingly put Jesus Christ to death again if it could. Our most hopeful moment comes when we recognize it is there, stop defending it, and begin to treat it as God directs.

Have you learned to recognize Haman within, even when he comes smiling and bowing and dripping with solicitude? When you have been relieved from a job in which you thought you were indispensable and no one even notices, do you feel slighted within, full of self-pity? Do you recognize Haman when your patience wears thin and you explode, saying something you wish you hadn't? Do you recognize your slimy friend when lust rises within and you keep it hidden from others, but allow the thoughts to dwell in your mind so that you can play with them?

This is the thing that put Jesus Christ on the cross and would do it again if it had the chance. This is our enemy. God alone knows how to end his trickery and defeat his evil purpose. He has already made his strategy known: It will be by means of a cross.

## Chapter 7

# THE PRICE OF SURVIVAL

We have now arrived at a moment of suspense and sinister possibilities. The collision course between Mordecai and Haman approaches its climax. Guided by Mordecai, Queen Esther is preparing the king for the revelation of Haman's real nature. It is a very ticklish matter. It is always a delicate thing to reveal the perfidy and treachery of some trusted friend—which is why Esther moves carefully and slowly. She has managed to awaken the king's curiosity and build up his sense of expectation. At the same time she has tricked Haman into dropping all subtlety so as to seek boldly and openly the destruction of Mordecai by nailing him to a gallows seventy-five feet high.

Chapter 6 of the biblical text opens with the king making a great discovery:

On that night the king could not sleep; and he gave orders to bring the book of memorable deeds, the chronicles, and they were read before the king. And it was found written how Mordecai had told about Bigthana and Teresh, two of the king's eunuchs, who guarded the threshold, and who had sought to lay hands upon King Ahasuerus. And the king said, "What honor or dignity has been bestowed on Mordecai for this?" The king's servants who attended him said, "Nothing has been done for him." (Esther 6:1–3)

Momentous events often hang upon seeming trivialities. Here is a restless king who cannot sleep, and because of that his empire is saved. Doubtless the king lay down on this night expecting to go right off to sleep, but his mind began to go over the events of the day, and he was curious and perplexed about Esther's behavior. Why had she come to him with this strange request, asking him to bring Haman to dinner the next day? And why, at the risk of her life, did she brave his disfavor to come? What is back of all this? His mind went over and over it. He tried to forget it, but he found himself coming back to it, tossing and turning restlessly. In the wee hours of the morning he decided to read something to get his mind off his thoughts, so he sent for the chronicles of the kingdom.

Perhaps you are saying, "Well, he certainly picked the right kind of book. I don't know what could be more dull and prosaic than the records of the kingdom. That kind of reading ought to put anyone to sleep." But these were not dull accounts. These were the records of memorable deeds, that is, true accounts of adventure and heroism. They were fascinating records of costly and daring achievements, exciting and significant history.

As these records were read, the king heard for the first time the story of Mordecai's loyalty toward him, when Mordecai had discovered the treachery of two of the king's trusted eunuchs. At considerable personal risk, he had reported the plot against the king's life to the queen, and she had in turn told the king. Though the king knew of the incident, he had not known of Mordecai's part in it. Not until the story was read to him early in the morning did he realize the unpaid debt he owed to Mordecai.

The discovery of this act of loyalty moved the king greatly. In these ancient days as even yet today, palace revolt was the scourge and fear of kings. November 22, 1963, stands as a grim reminder to us that even in safe America the assassination of a national leader is a dread possibility. Therefore, the king did not take this lightly, but was gripped by the sudden realization that he owed his very life and throne to Mordecai.

### Bought with a Price

Is there not a parallel to this in our Christian lives? In the Bible we have a record of memorable deeds. This book is the story of One who risked his life for us. In those dark hours upon the cross, Jesus entered into a death grapple with the powers of darkness that were against us. It is the most daring deed ever recorded in human history. There is nothing like it anywhere else in the records of mankind. One man, abandoned and alone, struggled with the invisible, stupefying forces of evil and conquered them for us.

It is this story which God uses to break through the stubborn willfulness of our hearts and make us realize that we are bought with a price. We owe our very lives to this man. John Wesley, until the day of his death, preserved a picture that someone had drawn him of the fire in the old rectory where he had once lived—the fire from which, as a boy of six, he had been rescued in the very nick of time. Beneath the picture in his own hand he had written the words, "Is not this a brand plucked from the burning?"

This is what the Holy Spirit brings before us when he wishes to awaken us to the fact that the flesh is not our friend, as we think, but an enemy. "You are not your own; you are bought with a price." The one you can trust is the one to whom you owe your life. It is this discovery of the right of Jesus Christ to our life which is the basis of all deliverance and victory. I do not mean some abstract acknowledgement that Christ died for us, or the recital of some orthodox creed. I mean the quiet realization that comes, perhaps in a communion service or when you are alone in your own home, when the truth breaks in upon you with shattering, staggering power that you are truly a brand plucked from the burning, that you have no right to a life of which he does not approve. In that moment of realization you discover that he who risked his life for you is your true friend.

This is a most significant moment for King Ahasuerus. He does not, as yet, know the true character of Haman, but for the first time he is made aware of the fact that Mordecai is his friend. He is deeply moved by this discovery and though it is yet early in the morning he hastens to display the gratitude he feels:

And the king said, "Who is in the court?" Now Haman had just entered the outer court of the king's palace to speak to the king about having Mordecai hanged on the gallows that he had prepared for him. So the king's servants told him, "Haman is there standing in the court." And the king said, "Let him come in." So Haman came in and the king said to him, "What shall be done to the man whom the king delights to honor?" (Esther 6:4–6)

Out of the king's discovery comes delight. Even though it is early in the morning he hastens to display the gratitude he feels. He asks, "Who is in the court?" By a strange twist of fate—one of those coincidences which are never coincidence —Haman is entering at that very moment to propose his bloody plan to the king. When the king greets him with the words, "What shall be done to the man whom the king delights to honor?", Haman has no doubt who that man is:

> And Haman said to himself, "Whom would the king delight to honor more than me?" And Haman said to the king, "For the man whom the king delights to honor, let royal robes be brought, which the king has worn, and the horse which the king has ridden, and on whose head a royal crown is set; and let the robes and the horse be handed over to one of the king's most noble princes; let him array the man whom the king delights to honor, and let him conduct the man on horseback through the open square of the city, proclaiming before him: 'Thus shall it be done to the man whom the king delights to honor.'" (Esther 6:6–9)

In the twisted mind of Haman there is only one man who he thinks can fit the description, "the man whom the king delights to honor,"—himself! How beautifully characteristic this is of the flesh in each of us. We feel we have an inherent right to the breaks in life. We are resentful and bitter when things do not go well. We feel we are being cheated of that which we eminently deserve. In our own estimation we have as much right to honor as the next fellow, and if we are passed by we leave the clear impression that sooner or later our superior qualities are bound to be recognized. That is the mind of the flesh.

## True Honor

But the remarkable thing here is that Haman well knows what true honor is. When we wish to honor someone we hold a testimonial dinner and give him a gold watch or a plaque to hang on the wall. But Haman knows there is something much better than that. Without hesitation he replies to the king, in effect, "Look, if you want to really honor this man in whom you delight, give him your kingly clothes to wear. Give him your personal horse to ride. Give him your own crown—in other words, give him yourself, publicly!"

That is true honor! Jesus said, "If any one serves me, the Father will honor him" (John 12:26). And the honor God gives is himself. God offers us his own clothing, his crown, all that he is. Do you honestly desire to honor the One to whom you owe your life? Then there is only one way you can do it. Give him your clothes to wear, give him your horse to ride, give him your crown. Give him authority in your life. Yield your members to him; as Paul said, "Present your bodies as a living sacrifice . . . to God" (Rom. 12:1). Grant him the right to be Lord over every area, every detail, every aspect of your life. That is what true honor is.

The next movement of the story is one of sardonic humor:

Then the king said to Haman, "Make haste, take the robes and the horse, as you have said, and do so to Mordecai the Jew who sits at the king's gate. Leave out nothing that you have mentioned." So Haman took the robes and the horse, and he arrayed Mordecai and made him ride through the open square of the city, proclaiming, "Thus shall it be done to the man whom the king delights to honor." Then Mordecai returned to the king's gate. But Haman hurried to his house, mourning and with his head covered. (Esther 6: 10–12)

What a scene this is! Imagine the bitter humiliation as Haman, in a blinding rage, walks through the streets of the city leading the horse of Mordecai who is clad in the royal garments of the king, wearing the royal crown upon his head. Can you imagine what must have gone through Haman's heart? All his plans of glory have fallen through. All his proud ambitions are threatened by this galling thing that he must do. Outwardly he is praising Mordecai, "This is the man whom the king delights to honor," but inwardly he is grinding his teeth with rage and awaiting a time of revenge.

But the whole point of the story is that he *does* this humiliating thing. In fact he will do anything as the price of survival. He is willing to stoop to any hypocrisy, any deceit, as long as he himself can stay in the seat of power. Left to itself, the flesh is openly arrogant, overbearing, boastful, lustful, cynical, proud. But when it is driven by the Spirit into a corner, it can assume a garb of righteousness. It becomes pious, religious, scrupulous about morals, zealous in church work, indignant over wrong, provokingly evangelical. Have you ever met Haman like this, walking through the streets of the city openly proclaiming, "This is the man whom the king delights to honor," but inwardly seething, hating, willing to do anything that looks good as long as it can survive?

Perhaps as a Christian you have discovered it is quite possible to look like you were serving Christ, but actually not do so. You can get by saying the right things, or going the right places with the right people, but inside you are still very much determined to have your own way and run your own life. Perhaps you have quarreled with someone and you know the Christian thing to do is to apologize and forgive; so you go through the motions, you say the words, but inside you vow you will never forget. That is the flesh—Haman—bowing to the demands of the king, but only because it is the price of survival to be a respectable Christian.

Haman will do anything. He will be scrupulously religious if he has to, anything as long as he can survive. The flesh can memorize Scripture, the flesh can teach Sunday school, the flesh can distribute tracts, give large gifts of money, give a stirring testimony, teach a Bible class, sing solos or preach a sermon. It can apologize after a fashion and repent to some extent and suffer with a martyred air. But there is one thing it will never do—it will never surrender, it will never change, it will never give up—never! It is a slippery, elusive thing and when backed into a corner it simply takes on a disguise and appears in a different form, but it is the same old deadly evil flesh. It would rather wreck your life than give up.

The righteousness of the flesh is always a counterfeit righteousness. It is centered in self and therefore it is always self-righteousness. Haman can seemingly honor Mordecai, but in fact he never really does. Thus the flesh can seemingly please God, but it never actually does. Romans 8:8 declares: "Those who are in the flesh cannot please God."

There is only one way the flesh can be overcome. It must be put to death. And when, in desperation, it is driven to turn religious and moral, its end may be very near. Haman has a premonition of this:

And Haman told his wife Zeresh and all his friends everything that had befallen him. Then his wise men and his wife Zeresh said to him, "If Mordecai, before whom you have begun to fall, is of the Jewish people, you will not prevail against him but will surely fall before him." While they were yet talking with him, the king's eunuchs arrived and brought Haman in haste to the banquet that Esther had prepared. (Esther 6:13–14)

One step yet remains to bring about Haman's defeat. Haman's slimy guise of friendship must be stripped from him in the presence of the king. The time for action has come. Thus Haman is brought "in haste" to the banquet Esther has prepared.

## Chapter 8

## HAMAN'S LAST SUPPER

The fateful moment has arrived. Nothing further can be done to deliver the kingdom from the evil influence of Haman until the king is made to see his true character. The moment for that revelation of evil has arrived:

So the king and Haman went in to feast with Queen Esther. And on the second day, as they were drinking wine, the king again said to Esther, "What is your petition, Queen Esther? It shall be granted you. And what is your request? Even to the half of my kingdom it shall be fulfilled." Then Queen Esther answered, "If I have found favor in your sight, O king, and if it please the king, let my life be given me at my petition, and my people at my request. For we are sold, I and my people, to be destroyed, to be slain, and to be annihilated. If we had been sold merely as slaves, men and women, I would have held my peace; for our affliction is not to be compared with the loss to the king." Then King Ahasuerus said to Queen Esther, "Who is he, and where is he, that would presume to do this?" And Esther said, "A foe and enemy! This wicked Haman!" (Esther 7:1–6)

73

Have you experienced this moment? Have you ever seen, in a God-given flash of insight, that the problem in your life is not the circumstances you live under, but the principle you have been living by? We call these "moments of truth" when suddenly we catch a glimpse of the way we look to others and are horrified by what we see. God opens our eyes to see that the evil attitude which we have been treating as a friend, defending, protecting, building little fences about, making excuses for, is not a friend and never has been. It is, in fact, the bitterest enemy we have.

This is the moment when we believe, perhaps for the first time, what the Scripture says concerning the natural life we have inherited from Adam—that it is totally worthless and no good thing dwells in it. What a shattering time this is! Haman the friend is revealed as Haman the traitor, the enemy, the double-dealing foe. When we see this, it is almost always followed by a time of struggle:

> Then Haman was in terror before the king and the queen. And the king rose from the feast in wrath and went into the palace garden; but Haman stayed to beg his life from Queen Esther, for he saw that evil was determined against him by the king. (Esther 7:6–7)

### Pacing in the Garden

Why does the king leave now that he knows who the real enemy is? Why doesn't he simply shout, "Off with his head!" like the queen in *Alice In Wonderland*? But he rises and goes off into the garden alone. You can see him pacing up and down, struggling with himself. He is angry at Haman and quite properly so. Haman knows this bodes no good for him, but the king is uncertain what to do. After all, Haman is the prime minister. He has deeply entrenched himself in the affairs of the kingdom. It is a radical step to execute a prime minister. It necessarily must involve a change in the whole pattern of life of the empire.

How do you feel when you finally see yourself in the wrong, perhaps after years of justifying and excusing yourself? Suddenly you see that the principle you have been living by has been the whole problem. But you know that to admit it and renounce it will mean a deep and radical adjustment on your part. Perhaps a deep-seated habit of life must be eradicated and the whole pattern of life will have to be changed. What do you do then?

It is always a shock to discover that it is not others' thoughtlessness that is the problem in our lives, as we fancied, but it is our own selfishness. It is not their malice; it is our lovelessness. It is shattering to realize that the actions we dislike in others are simply reactions to what we are doing to them. It isn't others' weaknesses; it is our relentless nagging of them. It isn't others' fickleness; it is our jealousy. It is our pretentious attitude of self-confidence and self-trust—or perhaps self-pity and self-excuse—that is the whole problem. What a struggle this revelation awakens within us. We are tempted to compromise, to smooth it over and go on, perhaps vowing to try a bit harder to control ourselves.

When the rich young ruler came to the Lord Jesus, the Lord quickly revealed that young man's heart and showed him that his love for what money could give possessed and owned his life. Then he said to him, "Go and sell all that thou hast and give to the poor and come and follow me." We read that the young man went away sorrowful, filled with struggle, unwilling to call that thing the enemy it was and cut it off sharply and completely. But the Lord, looking after him, was grieved because he loved him.

Like that young man, the king struggles with his feelings in the garden of the palace. At last he realizes there is only one possible escape from Haman's tyranny.

> And the king returned from the palace garden to the place where they were drinking wine, as Haman was falling on the couch where Esther was; and the king said, "Will he even assault the queen in my presence, in my own house?" As the words left the mouth of the king, they covered Haman's face. Then said Harbona, one of the eunuchs in attendance on the king, "Moreover, the gallows which Haman has prepared for Mordecai, whose word saved the king, is standing in Haman's house, fifty cubits high." And the king said, "Hang him on that." So they hanged Haman on the gallows which he had prepared for Mordecai. Then the anger of the king abated. (Esther 7:8–10)

When the king returns from the garden he sees Haman half-fallen on the queen's couch, clawing at her cravenly, pleading for mercy. The sight of it revolts and disgusts the king. With sarcasm he says, "Is he even trying to attack her in my very presence?" At that moment, a courtier standing by reminds him of the debt he owes to Mordecai. Pointing out the window he indicates the gallows which Haman had built for Mordecai, standing seventy-five feet high. In a flash the king sees the way out. Mordecai, the man whose word saved his life, shall be the new prime minister. So the king pronounces Haman's doom, "Hang him on that tree."

The moment the king gives the sentence of death, the evil power of Haman is ended. Thus, when you agree with God that the things of the flesh no longer have a right to live in your life, you will find deliverance from their power. In the language of Romans 6:11, this is to "consider yourselves dead to sin and alive to God in Christ Jesus."

## Another Supper

This chapter opened with an intimate supper in a private banqueting room, but it closed with a man nailed, screaming, to a tree until he is dead. Here is one of those timeless foreshadowings of the cross in the Old Testament. Centuries after this event another supper was held in a private banqueting room, upstairs in a building in Jerusalem. On that very similar occasion, three forces were represented. There were eleven disciples who did not know what was going on. Their hearts were troubled; they were concerned and perplexed, full of questions, ignorant and unknowing. And there was Jesus Christ their Lord, their Master, the perfect Son of Man, indwelt by the Father, aware of everything, fully awake to the danger of the hour and moving to avert the world's greatest disaster. And there also was Judas the traitor, intent only on fulfilling his own desire, ready to destroy everything if by hypocrisy and pretense he could get what he wanted, unconcerned for the terrible results that would follow his deed. That supper, too, ended with a man hanging upon a tree, nailed to a gallows. Wherever there is a cross in Scripture it is always for one purpose only—to put an evil man to death. That is what the cross will do in your life. That is what the cross of Jesus was—an instrument by which an evil man met death.

Does that shock you? Did you ever think of Jesus as an evil man? One of the most amazing sentences in all Scripture is that word in Paul's second letter to Corinthians, "For our sake he made him to be sin who knew no sin" (2 Cor. 5:21). That is, on the cross Jesus became Haman. Jesus was "made sin," made selfish, cruel, grasping, proud, cunning, slimy, evil; and when he was made sin, God's reaction was to put him to death, to nail him to a cross. That is the end of Haman! That is what the Bible says took place on the cross of our Lord Jesus. He became sin, and God put him to death.

Now what is true of a timeless event, such as the cross, becomes part of our experience when we reenact it in our own lives. This is why the cross of Jesus Christ, with all its possibilities of salvation and deliverance, can be an utterly useless thing as far as we are concerned if it is not translated into our experience. When we believe and act (that is what faith is—acting on the principles set forth in the cross) the cross becomes true in experience.

Once we learn this principle, we must act upon it daily. This is not the decision of a single moment, never to be repeated. It is a decision made again and again and again. Jesus said, "If any man would come after me, let him deny himself and take up his cross" (Matt. 16:24). How often must he take it up? "Daily." "Let him deny himself and take up his cross *daily*, and follow me."

"Hang it on that tree." That is the sentence that brings victory. No other way will work. It must be said every time Haman arises, for while we are in this body we are never delivered from the attempts of the flesh to influence us. But Haman need never be victorious, for if we believe what has been revealed about his nature, then without compromise or mercy we can look at this evil thing—jealousy, resentment, bitterness, malice, lust, self-confidence, pride, whatever it may be—and recalling that this is what put Jesus Christ to death and made Judas do what he did, and that this is what Jesus became when he took our place on the tree, we say, "Hang it on that tree."

When jealousy burns within you, hang it on the tree. When self-pity comes moaning and tempts you to feel sorry for yourself, hang it on the tree. When self-will rises up and says, "I am going to have my way. I don't care what others say," hang it on the tree. When resentment flames because we have been ignored or mistreated, hang it on that tree. When a critical spirit whispers some malicious thing, hang it on the tree. Say, "Lord Jesus, because I see this through your eyes as the evil thing it is, then standing here in the light of your cross, I put my will alongside yours and I agree it has no right to live. It must be put, in my experience, in the place where you put it in reality, the place of death." This is the only possible way to victory.

### The Right Man In

In the biblical text, a chapter division occurs at this point, but we must not stop here. The wrong man has now been toppled from his seat of power, but the right man must be brought in:

> On that day King Ahasuerus gave to Queen Esther the house of Haman, the enemy of the Jews. And Mordecai came before the king, for Esther had told what he was to her; and the king took off his signet ring, which he had taken from Haman, and gave it to Mordecai. And Esther set Mordecai over the house of Haman. (Esther 8:1–2)

This is a magic moment, full of possibilities. In your life, this is the moment when consciously and deliberately you reject the authority of self-interest and yield to the Holy Spirit the right to sovereign direction in all your concerns. Mordecai is brought in before the king, and the signet ring of authority is given to him. It is now possible for the wisdom and insight of Mordecai to manifest itself, through the authority of the king, throughout the entire empire. The moment we are ready to reject the authority of the flesh, we can give to the Spirit of God his rightful position as the prime minister of our kingdom.

This is sometimes called, in terms of human experience, "a second work of grace." It has also been called "full sanctification" or "the baptism of the Holy Spirit" or some other such term. It is often taken to be the true beginning of a Christian life and this has given rise to much confusion and misunderstanding in the apprehension of spiritual truth. It is quite wrong to look on this as though the Spirit of God were only now entering the life. You can see that Mordecai has been in the book of Esther right from the beginning, but it is only at this moment that he is brought before the king. This is the moment when the soul, the conscious life, becomes aware of the Spirit's right to rule in every area. But Mordecai has been there all along. He is not brought into the kingdom; he is brought before the king.

This is not, then, the baptism of the Holy Spirit. That takes place at the beginning of the Christian life, is never repeated, and is continually the basis from which God works in our lives. But this is what the New Testament calls "the filling of the Spirit." Since the task of the Holy Spirit is to make real in our lives the person of Jesus Christ, this could also picture the moment we consciously and with permanent intent yield to the Lordship of Jesus Christ. To yield to the

Lordship of Christ and to live a Spirit-filled life is exactly the same thing. These terms are interchangeable.

When we first yield conscious control of our kingdom to the Holy Spirit, we enter into a new experience in our lives. Our new Prime Minister sets about bringing everything in the kingdom under the authority we gave him, at the moment we place the signet ring of power upon his finger. This granting of authority may need to be reconfirmed in certain areas of our lives which we later discover are yet unsubmitted to him. For the strange thing about us is that we do not know ourselves. Though in some moment of dedication we may yield to the Spirit with all our heart and consciously grant him the right to rule, tomorrow we may discover there is another area that has not been brought under his control and this, too, must be submitted. When that occurs, we may have another experience of new advance similar to the first, so that it is possible to have many fillings of the Spirit. Each time, there is a return to the principle of dependence upon an indwelling Spirit for all activity.

### The Work of Mordecai

This is reflected in the wisdom Esther displays in handling the "house of Haman." Haman, the old prime minister, is now gone, but the sons of Haman are still around. The king gives Esther charge of them, and she immediately turns them over to Mordecai as the only one with the wisdom and knowledge to handle such a thorny matter properly.

You can recognize this in your own experience, if you are a Christian. You may come to the place where you know the truth about the flesh and believe that Christ's death has judged it within you; nevertheless, you discover evidence of the flesh still affecting you. Though the old man indeed has been hanged upon the tree, yet he still has, through the house of Haman, the ability to influence you, distract you, tempt you, and even defeat you. The answer to this is not to try to repress these influences by your will power. The king here makes no effort to try to overcome the house of Haman. He says, "It is your problem, Esther." And she, in turn, says to the Holy Spirit, "It is your problem. You handle the matter."

This is exactly what the New Testament tells us to do. We are to realize that our defense against the flesh will not be our own will power, our determination to control ourselves, but it will rather be a quiet resting upon the power of the Holy Spirit to handle the flesh whenever it appears, and an unrelenting dependence upon him to do so.

But, though Haman is gone, our problem is still not ended. Not only is the house of Haman still around, but there is that pesky edict that Haman tricked the king into signing, which still threatens the kingdom. What is to be done about this? It is the law of the Medes and the Persians and cannot be changed. How can disaster be averted?

# Chapter 9

# THE LAW OF THE
# SPIRIT

While evil Haman was still the prime minister he persuaded the king to sign an irrevocable law that permitted the armies of the land to destroy the Jews throughout the kingdom. Though Mordecai is now prime minister in Haman's place, the threat of the old law still hangs over the kingdom. A time has already been set for its execution, and that time inexorably draws nearer. The knowledge of this brings Esther in despair before the king again:

Then Esther spoke again to the king; she fell at his feet and besought him with tears to avert the evil design of Haman the Agagite and the plot which he had devised against the Jews. And the king held out the golden scepter to Esther, and Esther rose and stood before the king. And she said, "If it please the king, and if I have found favor in his sight, and if the thing seem right before the king, and I be pleasing in his eyes, let an order be written to revoke the letters devised by Haman the Agagite, the son of Hammedatha, which he wrote to destroy the Jews who are in all the provinces of the king. For how can I endure to see the

calamity that is coming to my people? Or how can I endure
to see the destruction of my kindred? (Esther 8:3–6)

As we have seen earlier in this book, the law of the Medes
and Persians which cannot be altered pictures in our own
experience what Romans calls, "the law of sin and death."
It, too, can never be altered or revoked while we are yet in
the body. It is this fact which produces a most baffling experience to the Christian. Though we have come to the place
where we recognize the evil of the flesh, our old Haman,
and refuse any longer to defend it (no longer excusing
our temper, impatience, resentment, self-righteousness, and
pride), and by that choice reenact in our experience the
meaning of the death of Christ for us, nevertheless we discover we are still not free to be what we want. Our efforts
to live a life that is pleasing to God still result in defeat and
barrenness.

It is this that baffles the apostle Paul as he describes his
experience in Romans 7: "I do not understand my own actions. For I do not do what I want, but I do the very thing
I hate. . . . I can will what is right, but I cannot do it."
(Rom. 7:15–18) Paul is saying here, "There was a time
when I didn't really know what God wanted. But I have
passed beyond that place. I now know what he wants and
I want very much to do it. There is no longer anything wrong
with my desire. I want desperately to please the Lord, but
when I try I discover that I am still under the control of
self." Paul's explanation for this experience is very important.
He says in effect, "I have discovered an unchangeable law at
work in my life that even my experience of the cross and the
resurrection has not eliminated—the law of sin and death. It

is this which is giving me this wretched, miserable experience."

## Who Will Deliver?

It is at this point in the experience of a growing Christian that he needs much help. His usual reaction is to feel there is something lacking in his dedication. So he consecrates himself to the Lord anew. Perhaps there is a service at the church and he goes forward, raises his hand, or bows his head and resolves again to serve the Lord better. He has discovered in experience what Paul means when he says, "I see in my members another law at war with the law of my mind and making me captive to the law of sin which dwells in my members. Wretched man that I am! Who will deliver me from this body of death?" (Rom. 7:23–24)

That is exactly what Queen Esther is saying at this point. Her cry, as she comes before the king the second time is: "Oh wretched woman that I am. Who will deliver me and my people from this law of sin and death which still has authority over us and holds us in its grip and power?"

The answer of the king to Esther is very revealing:

Then King Ahasuerus said to Queen Esther and to Mordecai the Jew, "Behold, I have given Esther the house of Haman, and they have hanged him on the gallows, because he would lay hands on the Jews. And you may write as you please with regard to the Jews, in the name of the king, and seal it with the king's ring; for an edict written in the name of the king and sealed with the king's ring cannot be revoked." (Esther 8:7–8)

Almost certainly the last statement of the king here should begin with the word, "but," rather than "for." It should read, "*but* an edict written in the name of the king and sealed with the king's ring cannot be revoked." The king is here declaring his utter bankruptcy to do anything about the law of destruction which still hangs over the people of Mordecai. He refers to the first edict that he had issued under Haman's instructions. He is saying, "I have done all I can. I have given you the house of Haman and ordered him hung upon the gallows, but I can do no more. The law of the Medes and the Persians cannot be changed. The matter is now in the hands of Mordecai." It is this utter helplessness on the part of the king and his readiness to admit it which is the great lesson the Holy Spirit thrusts upon us from this passage. The astonishing thing, which Paul says in Romans 7 he finally learned and which brought him to victory, was that his very efforts to please God by determined activity on his part only resulted in his becoming a carnal Christian! To his own amazement he discovered that the flesh does not only consist of obvious evil—impatience, worry, jealousy, pride, temper—but it also consists of much which he formerly thought to be good. He discovered that self-effort is also wrong and part of the flesh. Therefore, to set out to impress God by a demonstration of great zeal for his cause was to find himself utterly baffled and broken before the law of sin and death. He must learn at last that, "whatever does not proceed from faith is sin" (Rom. 14:23).

But King Ahasuerus makes no attempt at self-effort. Immediately he recognizes his total helplessness. He does the only wise thing; he puts the whole matter in Mordecai's hands. "Write whatever you please," he says, "and I will sign it." Without hesitation Mordecai acts:

The king's secretaries were summoned at that time, in the third month, which is the month of Sivan, on the twenty-third day; and an edict was written according to all that Mordecai commanded concerning the Jews to the satraps and the governors and the princes of the provinces from India to Ethiopia, a hundred and twenty-seven provinces, to every province in its own script and to every people in its own language, and also to the Jews in their script and their language. (Esther 8:9)

What is Mordecai's answer to this threat which hangs like the sword of Damocles over the kingdom? He cannot cancel out the old law; that is impossible. But there is one thing he can do. He can issue a new law, with the king's consent and authority, which would affect the farthest bounds of the kingdom, and which could turn the threatened defeat into victory. The details of the new law are now given us:

The writing was in the name of King Ahasuerus and sealed with the king's ring, and letters were sent by mounted couriers riding on swift horses that were used in the king's service, bred from the royal stud. By these the king allowed the Jews who were in every city to gather and defend their lives, to destroy, to slay, and to annihilate any armed force of any people or province that might attack them, with their children and women, and to plunder their goods, upon one day throughout all the provinces of King Ahasuerus, on the thirteenth day of the twelfth month, which is the month of Adar. A copy of what was written was to be issued as a decree in every province, and by proclamation to all peoples, and the Jews were to be ready on that day to avenge themselves upon their enemies. So the couriers, mounted on their swift horses that were used in the king's service, rode out in

haste, urged by the king's command; and the decree was
issued in Susa the capital. (Esther 8:10–14)

Here is a new law that gave the Jews authority to act
over all their enemies. The first law could not be eliminated,
but its effects could be cancelled out. So we read in Romans
8:2, "The law of the Spirit of life in Christ Jesus has set me
free from the law of sin and death." Again in Galatians Paul
says in triumph, "It is no longer I who live, but Christ who
lives in me" (Gal. 2:20.). That is, the law of his life in me
is able to counteract the effects of sin and death. It is no
longer I who work, but it is he who works in me. And so I
live his life. It is still I who live it, but I live it by faith in
the Son of God who loved me and gave himself for me.
When I count on his indwelling life to work through me,
he turns even my failures into victories. The very circumstances of defeat become the stairway to triumph.

### Transmuted Tears

"Your sorrow will turn into joy," the Lord Jesus said to his
disciples before he went to the cross (John 16:20). He did
not say, "Your sorrow shall be replaced by joy." That is the
best we can hope for in the world's perspective. We look for
a change of circumstances by which we can move from sorrow into joy. But Jesus is saying, "The very thing which
causes you sorrow, when the Holy Spirit comes into your
life will be the very thing in which you find joy." Your sor-
rows shall be translated, transmuted into joy. How right he
was! The shadow of the cross had stricken their hearts with
fear and caused deep sorrow. They could see it as nothing
but pain, anguish, and heartache. But Jesus pointed out that

when the Spirit came that very cross would be the source of their richest joy. And so it proved to be.

Thus the law of sin and death may continue to work in our circumstances, but the law of the Spirit of life in Christ Jesus transmutes those very painful circumstances into rejoicing and blessing. Paul learned this when he found one day a thorn in his flesh—a raw, grinding, unpleasant thing from which he struggled to be free. He asked three times to have it taken away, but the answer came, "My grace is sufficient for you." Grasping that answer, he realized that the thorn made him feel weak and helpless, and it was his sense of weakness which caused him to cast himself upon the sustaining grace of an indwelling Lord. That, in turn, resulted in a mighty display of the power of God in his ministry. So Paul could say, "I will all the more gladly boast of my weaknesses, that the power of Christ may rest upon me" (2 Cor. 12:9).

So the new law of the Spirit never eliminates the law of sin and death; it simply superimposes upon it a higher power. Some time ago, as a growing boy, I discovered that something was happening to my eyes. I could not see as well as other boys. Finally I checked with an eye doctor, and he informed me that I was suffering from the law of myopia, that is, the law of nearsightedness. No matter how hard I tried, I could not see as well as others. I would squint and peer and strain, but all my efforts did me no good. I simply could not see what others saw. I was suffering from a law in my members which held me under bondage.

But some time later I discovered a new law. It is called the law of contact lenses! I was told that if I would allow two tiny bits of plastic, no bigger than the end of my finger, to be inserted into my eyes, I would be able to see perfectly. The new law would counteract the law of myopia. I am happy to say that I believed that propaganda and made the experiment. The result was instant, perfect vision which has continued ever since.

Now the law of myopia is still at work, and any time I think it has been overcome for good I need only take the plastic lenses from my eyes, and I discover I go right back into the same helplessness of vision. But whenever I quietly reckon upon the law of contact lenses and insert them into my eyes, there is nothing more I need to do. I don't have to think about them again for long periods of time. They are constantly at work overcoming the law of nearsightedness and giving me perfect vision.

### Joy of Anticipation

But to return to our story. When the new edict was announced throughout the kingdom, there was great joy and gladness:

Then Mordecai went out from the presence of the king in royal robes of blue and white, with a great golden crown and a mantle of fine linen and purple, while the city of Susa shouted and rejoiced. The Jews had light and gladness and joy and honor. And in every province and in every city, wherever the king's command and his edict came, there was gladness and joy among the Jews, a feast and a holiday. (Esther 8:15–17)

Note, this joy comes even before the deliverance has actually been realized. It has simply been announced; it has not yet been experienced. Mordecai and the Jews are now honored everywhere. The city of Susa shouts with gladness.

When it breaks upon our defeated hearts that God has made a way out of the barrenness of mere fleshly activity, we know instant joy. What a relief it is! Compare this edict of Mordecai's with that of Haman's in chapter 3. The result in the city when Haman's edict was announced was one of confusion and bewilderment. But now Mordecai is in power, and when the new edict is issued there is joy and gladness, feasting and holiday. What a glorious thing it is to realize that deliverance is possible; that this miserable, barren, unfruitfulness is not God's intended experience for us; that each one of us, without exception, is free to step into the glorious reality of a life lived in the power of the Spirit of God, for God is no respecter of persons.

How well I recall the night when, as a young man in the service of the United States Navy, I was standing watch in a building in Pearl Harbor. It was my duty to be on watch for four hours, from two A.M. to six A.M. During those hours I could write letters, read, or otherwise fill my time as long as I remained on duty and awake. I had brought with me William R. Newell's great book, *Romans Verse by Verse*. As I read the words of Romans 6:14 they hit me with peculiar force. "Sin will have no dominion over you, since you are not under law but under grace." I had been struggling with so many things in my life which were holding me back, baffling me, mocking me. Those words seemed to come to life. They leaped out from the page and came thundering at me. "Sin will have no dominion over you"! I did not understand the process by which victory would come, but my faith laid hold of those words. Though I had not yet experienced deliverance, I walked up and down the floor with my heart overflowing with victorious joy. Here was the word of the Holy Spirit that the things which made for defeat in my life would utterly be broken. Looking back through the years since I can see that the promise of that hour has been fulfilled. The hindering shackles have been broken away by the power of the indwelling life of Jesus Christ. But even before I actually walked in victory I knew the joy of it by anticipation when the promise came home to my heart in power.

Not only was there joy in the kingdom of Persia when Mordecai's edict was announced, but there was also another remarkable result. "And many from the peoples of the country declared themselves Jews, for the fear of the Jews had fallen upon them" (v. 17). This simply means that pagan Gentiles, seeing the Jews so joyous and confident in Mordecai's wisdom and power, gave up their paganism and turned to the only true God. For the first time they noticed something real about these Jews. Suddenly these people had come to life, and there was a glorious quality of joy and faith about them that made their neighbors say, "There must be something wonderful about this faith in Jehovah." And they too became Jews!

When, because of your faith, your life too becomes perceptibly different; when your reactions are quite opposite to what the situation seems to call for and your activities can no longer be explained in terms of your personality; that is when your neighborhood will sit up and take notice. In the eyes of the world, it is not our relationship with Jesus Christ that counts; it is our resemblance to him! In the midst of circumstances that look like certain defeat, there is no more powerful testimony than the joy produced by faith.

Chapter 10

# THE SWEET TASTE OF VICTORY

Throughout the book of Esther reference has been continually made to a specific day and hour when the principles represented by the edict of Haman and that of Mordecai shall clash headlong. That day has now arrived:

Now in the twelfth month, which is the month of Adar, on the thirteenth day of the same, when the king's command and edict were about to be executed, on the very day when the enemies of the Jews hoped to get the mastery over them, but which had been changed to a day when the Jews should get the mastery over their foes, the Jews gathered in their cities throughout all the provinces of King Ahasuerus to lay hands on such as sought their hurt. (Esther 9:1-2)

God has appointed a day when what we have learned intellectually through the study of the Word of God, illuminated by the Holy Spirit, must be put to the test in the hurly-burly and mud and blood of life. Though our hearts may be filled with joy when we learn of the possibility of total deliverance from the bondage of the flesh, the day must come when we go back to the place of pressure, to the cir-

cumstances of former defeat, where our head knowledge will
be put to the test. God is forever conducting examinations.
Life is not merely an exercise in mental acrobatics. No
principle of victory is of any real value unless it can be lived
out in the reality of daily experience.

So, like the Jews, we must come to the actual day of combat. When the moment of temptation is upon us, when the
pressure is great to give way to the flesh, what do we do? We
can now trace in our story the process of appropriation,
the means by which the provision for victory is applied to the
specific time of combat. There is first the authority of faith!

> And no one could make a stand against them, for the fear
> of them had fallen upon all peoples. All the princes of the
> provinces and the satraps and the governors and the royal
> officials also helped the Jews, for the fear of Mordecai had
> fallen upon them. (Esther 9:2-3)

Under the edict of Haman the people were literally commanded to fight against the Jews, and under that edict the
Jews were forbidden to defend themselves. Any effort they
made in their own defense was a violation of the law of the
land. The very law itself was against them, and they could
not fight back legally. Thus we read in Romans 7, "While we
were living in the flesh, our sinful passions, aroused by the
law, were at work in our members to bear fruit for death."
(Rom. 7:5) That simply means that when we Christians
endeavor to please God by our self-directed activities in his
behalf, without dependence upon the life of Christ within,
and we go on our own steam, the result is that our sinful
passions within are aroused by the law we are trying to obey.
Have we not often felt this? Someone tells us not to do some-

thing, and immediately we want to do that very thing. Our sinful passions are aroused by the prohibition of the law. The very law that commands our obedience also arouses our resentment against it.

## No Longer Outlaws

But now a second edict has been issued. The edict from Mordecai set the Jews free so that now in their fighting they would no longer be outlaws or criminals. They can now fight with the full authority of the throne behind them. Thus in Romans 7:6 we read, "But now we are discharged from the law, dead to that which held us captive, so that we serve not under the old written code but in the new life of the Spirit." We now have God's full authority to stand on the basis of an imparted life—the life of the Lord Jesus made real to us by an indwelling Spirit. We are now to realize that we have full authority to withstand every manifestation of the flesh. We must no longer use the excuse, "I can't help doing this; after all, I'm only human." It is to free us from the effects of this fallen "humanity" that the Holy Spirit has assumed the place of power in our lives.

But note, also, that "all the princes of the provinces and the satraps and the governors and the royal officials also helped the Jews." The authority of faith is such that as we walk out on this great principle of activity, even the very circumstances we thought were against us now combine to help us on to victory. When Joseph was sold into slavery, put into prison, and from there exalted to second place in the kingdom of Egypt, his brethren, who had sold him, came to Egypt to seek relief from famine. When Joseph made himself known to them they were very much afraid. But to comfort them. Joseph said a wonderful thing: "You meant evil against me; but God meant it for good" (Gen. 50:20). Thus the very circumstances that we blame for defeating us and bringing us into bondage are often the very thing that God uses to help us to victory. I have often wondered what those Christians in Damascus must have thought when they saw being led by the hand that poor, blinded Saul of Tarsus who had come there breathing out threats and slaughter against them and from whom they were now hiding in fear of their lives. But he had now come to be on their side. God had arrested the arrester and brought him a captive to them. Of course they were afraid and couldn't trust him at first, but gradually they saw that by the might of glory and grace, God had transformed their greatest enemy into their greatest defender. What a picture this is of what happens in the life of one who understands the victory that God has planned.

But there is yet more to the pattern of victory. There is not only the authority of faith; there is also dependence upon the man of power:

> For Mordecai was great in the king's house, and his fame spread throughout all the provinces; for the man Mordecai grew more and more powerful. So the Jews smote all their enemies with the sword, slaughtering, and destroying them, and did as they pleased to those who hated them. (Esther 9:4–5)

These Jews were now fighting in the consciousness that the man of power was on their side. The power in which they fought was not their own, but came right from the throne itself. Thus they were simply irresistible in their fighting. Each of these Jews was saying, as we must learn to say,

"I can't; but He can; therefore I can!" Power flows from the very throne of the universe itself when we act on that principle.

Not long ago I saw in a magazine a picture of a straw that had been picked up by a tornado and driven through a telephone pole. There was also an iron fire hydrant that had been pierced by several slivers of wood. How could this happen? If I gave you a straw and said, "Would you kindly go out and drive this through a telephone pole?", you would say it was impossible. But it has actually happened. The explanation is that the weak straw was caught up in the power of a tornado, and in the power of that mighty wind, it was able to do that which it could never do by itself. Thus, in the power of the mighty Wind of God we can do all that needs to be done. It won't always be to put straws through telephone poles. The Holy Spirit will never be like a tornado if all we need is a gentle breeze. But if we need a tornado, that is what he will be. There is nothing we need to appropriate this other than the authority of faith and dependence upon his royal power to bring to pass all that he intends.

### Marks of Victory

The next movement of this story brings before us certain marks of victory. How can we really know that we are walking in the Spirit? There are certain indelible marks, impossible to imitate, by which we can know that we have found the principle of victory. Four of these marks are given to us here. The first is the slaying of the ten sons of Haman:

> In Susa the capital itself the Jews slew and destroyed five hundred men, and also slew Parshandatha and Dalphon and

Aspatha and Poratha and Adalia and Aridatha and Parmashta and Arisai and Aridai and Vaizatha, the ten sons of
Haman the son of Hammedatha, the enemy of the Jews;
but they laid no hand on the plunder. (Esther 9:6–10)

In the original Hebrew these ten sons of Haman are listed
here in a most striking way. Their names do not follow one
another across the page, as they appear in the English text,
but are listed in a column. In such a form they stand right
out from the page. In a parallel column at the other side of
the page, opposite each of the names of Haman's sons, the
Hebrew word "self" is repeated. Thus the word "self" is
linked with the meaning of each name right down the
column.

These ten names have most interesting meanings. Some
of them are of Persian derivation and their significance difficult to determine, but the following meanings are generally
accepted: *Parshandatha* means "Curious Self," that is, nosi-
ness, a busy-body in other people's matters. This characteristic of the flesh is slain by the power of the Spirit. *Dalphon*
means "Weeping Self" or self-pity, picturing the remarkable
ability we have to feel sorry for ourselves. This, too, is put
to death. *Aspatha* means "Assembled Self," self-mobilized for
its own ends or self-sufficiency. *Poratha* means "Generous
Self," but in the bad sense intended here it indicates spend-
thriftiness, impulsive buying for the sake of self. *Adalia*
means "Weak Self," or the feeling of inferiority, self-con-
sciousness.

*Aridatha* means "Strong Self," that is, assertiveness, the
insistence on one's own way. *Parmashta* means "Preeminent
Self." This suggests ambition, that which desires to have
preeminence over others. *Arisai* means "Bold Self" or im-

pudence. *Aridai* means "Dignified Self," which again in a bad sense is pride or haughtiness, a sense of superiority. The last name, *Vaizatha*, is the worst of all. It means "Pure Self," that is, self-righteousness, the self which considers itself purer than everyone else.

All of these were put to death. They were refused the right to live. The disappearance of these traits of the self-life is the first great evidence of having discovered the secret of victory.

## Double Victory

The second mark is the double victory recorded in the capital city:

> That very day the number of those slain in Susa the capital was reported to the king. And the king said to Queen Esther, "In Susa the capital the Jews have slain five hundred men and also the ten sons of Haman. What then have they done in the rest of the king's provinces! Now what is your petition? It shall be granted you. And what further is your request? It shall be fulfilled." And Esther said, "If it please the king, let the Jews who are in Susa be allowed tomorrow also to do according to this day's edict." (Esther 9:11–13)

On the thirteenth day of the twelfth month, in exact accord with the edicts of Haman and Mordecai, the great conflict occurred throughout the one hundred and twenty-seven provinces of the kingdom. But in the capital city of Susa, by special request of Esther, the slaughter was extended another full day to include the fourteenth, so the victory in the capital was double that in the provinces. When the law of the Spirit of life has set us free from the law of sin and death so that the self-manifestations cease, there will be rejoicing and gladness among all our friends and associates throughout the kingdom of our influence. We will be so much easier to live with! But they will not know the half of it. The joy of release in our own hearts will be at least double that which others experience by our victory. One dear woman said, "No one can ever possibly know the glorious sense of relief that I have experienced in being set free from the chains of self. Others see the happiness I experience, but only I know the fullness of joy within!"

### A Public Disclosure

The third unmistakable mark of the fullness of the Spirit is the public display of the ten sons of Haman. Esther's request to the king continues:

> "And let the ten sons of Haman be hanged on the gallows."
> So the king commanded this to be done; a decree was issued
> in Susa, and the ten sons of Haman were hanged. (Esther
> 9 13–14)

These evil offspring of Haman had already been slain, but now Esther requests that their dead bodies be publicly displayed. There is no clearer sign of the victory of the Spirit than when a believer find himself willing to share with others the story of his battle with the ugliness of self, and to encourage them in the true way of victory. If we attempt to control the flesh by willpower, the last thing we want is to have anyone know we have problems of such a nature. But let us begin to walk in the Spirit and we become quite willing for anyone to know the character of these struggles. The skeletons come out of our closets. We no longer fear discovery, for the end of these self traits is obvious to all.

## Hands Off

The last mark of true victory is three times mentioned in this account. Wherever the Jews fought, though they defeated their enemies on every hand, it is everywhere recorded of them, "they laid no hands on the plunder." They did not take advantage of the victory to enrich themselves. They were not interested in personal advancement as a result of this remarkable turn of events. This is a clear mark of genuine spiritual victory. There are always some Christians who wish to be free from certain problems in their disposition because it will mean a chance for advancement in employment, or it will improve conditions at home. Perhaps they hope to get along better with their mothers-in-law! But the mark of true victory is that you don't care a whit what happens to you, you want victory simply because it is God's desire for you. A woman wrote in *Decision* magazine, "Such a short time ago I was afraid of doing wrong because it might hurt me. Now I am beginning to feel it is more important not to hurt my Father." Such an attitude precludes all parade of piety, avoids any seeking for the admiration of others. The delivered heart quickly rejoices in the sweetness of victory, but makes no attempt to turn it to its own advantage.

The next section of the text repeats again and again the words *rest, feasting, gladness, holiday-making, concern for others*, and *gifts*:

This was on the thirteenth day of the month of Adar, and on the fourteenth day they rested and made that a day of

feasting and gladness. But the Jews who were in Susa gathered on the thirteenth day and on the fourteenth, and
rested on the fifteenth day, making that a day of feasting
and gladness. Therefore the Jews of the villages, who live in
the open towns, hold the fourteenth day of the month of
Adar as a day for gladness and feasting and holiday-making,
and a day on which they send choice portions to one another. And Mordecai recorded these things, and sent letters
to all the Jews who were in all the provinces of King
Ahasuerus, both near and far, enjoining them that they
should keep the fourteenth day of the month Adar and also
the fifteenth day of the same, year by year, as the days
on which the Jews got relief from their enemies, and as the
month that had been turned for them from sorrow into
gladness and from mourning into a holiday; that they
should make them days of feasting and gladness, days for
sending choice portions to one another and gifts to the
poor. (Esther 9:17–22)

Note how frequently the character of the celebration of this
day is emphasized. It was to be a day of feasting and gladness (vv. 17, 18, 19, and twice again in v. 22). It was to be
a day of rest. It was to be a day of holiday-making, of enjoying what was accomplished. It was a day in which they ob-
tained relief from their enemies. It was a day of showing
generosity and deep concern for others, of sending gifts to
the poor. All this indicates the results of the victory that was
accomplished. What is this but the enjoyment of the fruit of
the Spirit?

How much did the kingdom of Persia experience these
blessings while Haman was in the prime minister's seat?
None whatever! When Haman ruled, the result in the kingdom was confusion, mourning, weeping, dejection, and de-

spair. How aptly this describes the experience of a Christian who is earnestly struggling to do his best for God, but has never yet learned what God wants to teach him in terms of a rest and dependence upon the indwelling life of the Lord Jesus to work through him.

Care needs to be exercised at this point. We are so used to looking to our circumstances as the source of happy feelings, that when we hear that we can experience rest, gladness, and concern for others continually, we instinctively feel that somehow that means we will have happy circumstances all the time. We must be careful to understand exactly what is offered. The promised supply of peace, victory, joy and a continual out-flowing river of love does not necessarily mean that there will be a change in our circumstances. Victory does not mean freedom from weariness, sickness, sorrow, heart-ache, pressure, defeat, or danger in the Christian's experience. Rather, in the midst of these things we shall, at the same time, experience a quiet inner joy, a sense of sustaining strength, and a freedom from the manifestations of self-life.

The Lord warned, "In the world you have tribulation; but be of good cheer, I have overcome the world" (John 16:33). There is a place of relief and release despite the circumstances. Deliverance comes not by a change of our conditions, but by another principle, the continual imparting to us by the Holy Spirit of the indwelling life of the risen Lord whose adequate resources maintain our spirits despite the circumstances.

Now in the summary of this book we have the steps outlined for us for the "how" of victory:

So the Jews undertook to do as they had begun, and as Mordecai had written to them. For Haman the Agagite, the son of Hammedatha, the enemy of all the Jews, had plotted against the Jews to destroy them, and had cast Pur, that is the lot, to crush and destroy them, but when Esther came before the king, he gave orders in writing that his wicked plot which he had devised against the Jews should come upon his head, and that he and his sons should be hanged on the gallows. (Esther 9:23–25)

Every Christian who knows Jesus Christ as an indwelling life stumbles occasionally into victory. The Spirit of God puts us in circumstances where we are overwhelmed and in the moment of desperation we cry out to God for help. Inevitably when we do that we experience deliverance, victory. This is emergency help, requested only when we get our backs up against the wall. But the normal condition of a believer is that we are always to be in this condition, always experiencing in the body the dying of the Lord Jesus, that the power of Christ may rest upon us. When we learn to walk in the consistent knowledge that this is our true condition, then we become consistent in our experience of victory.

### In a Nutshell

The first step, we are reminded, was the exposure of Haman. His name is given to us in full, Haman the Agagite. Remember, Agag was the king of the Amalekites, against whom God has pronounced eternal enmity. Agag was opposed to all God wanted to do. So here is Haman the Agagite, the son of Hammedatha, the enemy of all the Jews, and his perfidy, treachery, and subtlety are now fully exposed. So also, the first step in deliverance from the Haman within us is to learn to recognize him. But this is far more difficult than it sounds. We justify the things that are destroying us and make excuses for them, calling them sweet-sounding names and thus putting honey and syrup labels on bottles of poison. That makes them all the more deadly, doesn't it? No wonder it is difficult to recognize the voice of the devil in our experience.

The second step is the knowledge that a new decree has been issued: "But when Esther came before the king, he gave orders in writing that his wicked plot which he had devised against the Jews should come upon his [Haman's] own head" (v. 25). The new decree meant that the Jews were set free from the law of the old decree. For us, this pictures that law of a new life in Jesus Christ, dwelling within us, which sets us free from the law of sin and death in our experience. Christ is in us and he, therefore, becomes our resource. It is no longer up to us to try to do our best. It is up to us now to trust him to do his best through us. What a difference that is! It is the difference between trying to show the world how much we can do for Christ and letting him show the world what he can do through us. It isn't a struggle now to try to be good, but by depending upon the One who is good, who dwells within us, we step forward to do what needs to be done, and his life becomes manifest in terms of our activity. The knowledge of this is the second step to victory.

And then the third thing is the hanging of Haman and his sons on the gallows. The amazing thing is that until we are willing to put the old life with its manifestations in the place of death where God put it in Jesus Christ, we never can lay hold of that indwelling life. When we try to make both Haman and Christ live at the same time, keeping a portion of the ego as a pet area from which we exclude God, we find we cannot lay hold of his life in us. Victory comes

when we are content to have our egos overlooked and humili-
ated if need be, that the life of Jesus may be manifested and
expressed through us—that his self-giving may replace our
self-seeking. When we are content to have it that way, not
only in terms of words, but in terms of experience, then
there is an immediate experience of his risen life flowing
through us, working everything out. That is victory.

The chapter ends with the establishment of the feast of
Purim:

> Therefore they called these days Purim, after the term Pur
> [the lot]. And therefore, because of all that was written in
> this letter, and of what they had faced in this matter, and
> of what had befallen them, the Jews ordained and took it
> upon themselves and their descendants and all who joined
> them, that without fail they would keep these two days ac-
> cording to what was written and at the time appointed
> every year, that these days should be remembered and kept
> throughout every generation, in every family, province, and
> city, and that these days of Purim should never fall into
> disuse among the Jews, nor should the commemoration of
> these days cease among their descendants. Then Queen
> Esther, the daughter of Abihail, and Mordecai the Jew gave
> full written authority, confirming this second letter about
> Purim. Letters were sent to all the Jews, to the hundred and
> twenty-seven provinces of the kingdom of Ahasuerus, in
> words of peace and truth, that these days of Purim should
> be observed at their appointed seasons, as Mordecai the Jew
> and Queen Esther enjoined upon the Jews, and as they had
> laid down for themselves and for their descendants, with re-
> gard to their fasts and their lamenting. The command of
> Queen Esther fixed these practices of Purim, and it was
> recorded in writing. (Esther 9:26–32)

Even today the Jews celebrate this story of Esther in the feast of Purim. They set aside two days for holiday, feasting, gladness and merrymaking. On the first evening they read through the story of Esther. This is the day when all Jewish children come into their own. They bring noise makers, little drums and horns to the service, and whenever the name of Haman is mentioned, they blow the horns and pound on the drums, booing and hissing through the reading of the book wherever Haman is mentioned. The second day is set aside for feasting and merrymaking, and for exchanging gifts, very much as we celebrate Christmas. All of this is in remembrance of the deliverance accomplished by Esther and Mordecai in the days of the Persian Empire, some five hundred years before Christ. It is celebrated to this day because God wants the Jewish people never to forget this deliverance. It is to be forever a very important day in their history.

### Continual Victory

There is a tradition among the Jews that the feast of Purim is the only feast that will be observed after the Messiah comes. The feasts of Tabernacles and Passover and all others will cease, they say, when the Messiah comes. But the feast of Purim will go on even in the days of the kingdom of God on earth. This reflects the truth that to walk in the Spirit is normal for both time and eternity. We must teach it to our descendants as well that our children may see what it means to walk in victory over resentment, jealousy, impatience, envy, lust, self-love, self-seeking, pride, self-pity, and all other experiences of the self-life. So many of our children grow up in Christian homes and yet go out bewildered, bored, frus-

trated, unhappy, not enjoying what they have because we
who are parents have not learned to walk in the Spirit. It is
a walk, a continual process of taking the same steps over
and over, every time conflict comes, until there is a manifestation of continual victory.

That is what Enoch learned. We are told that Enoch lived
sixty-five years before he learned to walk with God. I wonder
if it will take some of us that long. After he learned to walk
he walked three hundred years with God until one day, as a
little girl once said, "God just said to him, 'Come on, Enoch,
come on home with me. It's too far to go back.'" So he was
not, because God took him. He walked on into glory. That is
the picture of what God would have for the believer in Christ.

The book closes on one last point God wants us to remember:

> King Ahasuerus laid tribute on the land and on the coast-
> lands of the sea. And all the acts of his power and might,
> and the full account of the high honor of Mordecai, to
> which the king advanced him, are they not written in the
> Book of the Chronicles of the kings of Media and Persia?
> For Mordecai the Jew was next in rank to King Ahasuerus,
> and he was great among the Jews and popular with the mul-
> titude of his brethren, for he sought the welfare of his
> people and spoke peace to all his people. (Esther 10:1–3)

Here is the same king and the same kingdom with which the
book began. The only difference is that Haman is out and
Mordecai is in. But what a difference! Mordecai "sought the
welfare of the people and spoke peace to all." Just as the
king and the kingdom remain the same, so the Christian remains the same person when the Spirit is granted the place
of control. Personality does not change, but is cleansed and

enhanced by the presence of the Spirit. So Paul can say, "I am crucified with Christ: nevertheless I live." The person remains the same; the principle upon which he lives and acts is entirely different. "Not I, but Christ lives in me" (Gal. 2:20, kjv). This is the secret. This is the Spirit-filled life. As Mordecai, through the will of the king, brings power and peace to the kingdom, so the Spirit, through our will and never beyond it, brings peace and prosperity into our lives.

This is why the Spirit-led Christian can fall into a cesspool of circumstances and come up smelling like a rose. Disappointments make him better, not bitter. Heartaches become sources of joy. Hard circumstances produce in him the choicest of virtues. The weaker he feels, the more impact his life has on others. He becomes sweeter, mellower, filled with an inner beauty. Paul describes his own experience in these beautiful words: "But thanks be to God, who in Christ always leads us in triumph, and through us spreads the fragrance of the knowledge of him everywhere." (2 Cor. 2:14)

Have you found this great secret? Have you learned to count upon an indwelling Spirit to meet every demand made upon you with wholly adequate resources? Perhaps you would like to pray that Paul's experience might also be yours, as we end this study together.